RECKLESS

MERCY

A TROPHY OF GOD'S GRACE

CARL TUTTLE

COACHING SAINTS
PUBLICATIONS
WWW.COACHINGSAINTS.COM

Printed in the United States of America

Published by Coaching Saints Publications

Layout, cover design: Brian Blount
wwww.webvisiongraphics.com

DEDICATION

To my children, the six most important people in my life:

I would hate to have gone through life without you. The recent events I've experienced have made it clearer than ever how very important you are and how much you mean to me.

I hope that through reading this book, you will learn a little bit more about your old man and my struggles to remain faithful to my relationship with Jesus. I want you to know that it's been hard but also well worth it.

Zachary, Noah, Mercy, Sophie, Carlton, and Lucy—this book is dedicated to you.

ENDORSEMENTS

Wow! Carl Tuttle's new book is a vulnerable, real, raw picture of his life. I loved it. Through his vulnerability, he actively engages us, the readers, in the lessons he learned through various parts of his own spiritual and human journey, as well as what happened behind a historical church movement, the Vineyard. This insight could have only come from an insider like himself. I loved hearing from his vantage point and experiencing his honesty in telling readers who he was. Carl shares his sometimes traumatic backstory without making excuses about the choices he made as a result. This made me want to really dig into the overall message of what he has given us in this work.

Whether you have heard of the Vineyard Movement before or you are just a student of Christian life process, this book will take you to a place that few authors dare to share. Carl exhibited a level of self-awareness and openness that I am so proud of him for instilling in this book! *Reckless Mercy* will help you grow as a person and take risks as a Christian while maybe even finding your own healing process in this story.

Shawn Bolz, author of *Translating God*, *God Secrets*, and *Growing Up With God*

I could not put this book down. It has everything! It's heartbreakingly honest, vulnerable, funny, and full of wisdom and insight, just like Carl. I loved it. *Reckless Mercy* includes timeless gems of teaching written in a humble, accessible way. I want every broken person to read this and find hope. I want everyone who seeks to bring God's love to broken people to read this and discover the sheer kindness of grace. In other words, I want everyone to read this!

Mike Pilavachi, Co-founder of Soul Survivor,
UK

Reckless Mercy is the heart-wrenching, hope-giving story of the Vineyard Movement's favorite prodigal son. My second favorite thing about this book is that Carl owns his own stuff. He pulls no punches about his own brokenness. There is not an ounce of pretense or blame shifting in the man. I love that about him. He has taught me so much about authenticity and genuine repentance. But that's only my second favorite thing about the book.

My favorite thing is that Carl doesn't glorify authenticity, like so many in our day. He glorifies the redeeming power of mercy that compels us on from brokenness to wholeness. I've seen this at work in Carl's life in the indisputable restoration of relationships, calling, and legacy. Having a front row seat to the unfolding of Carl's story has been one of God's greatest gifts to me as a pastor. It has persuaded me afresh that the gospel really works. And that's why *Reckless Mercy* is a must-read, not just for Vineyard folk, but for every soul in need of gospel hope, prodigal or not.

Alan Frow, Lead Pastor of Southlands Church,
Brea, CA

Reckless Mercy is a book by my friend, Carl Tuttle, that will show you how God's kindness stretches far beyond anything we can understand naturally. Through Carl's story, you will see how God never stops pursuing us and His callings are never-ending.

Robby Dawkins, author, international conference speaker, and equipper

Get ready for a journey. Carl Tuttle's account of a fifty-year pilgrimage is authentic, sad, invigorating, and, most of all, a signpost to the great love of God. Reading it made me think of an old Robert Redford movie, *Jeremiah Johnson*. At the end of a long season in a mountainous, challenging, and dangerous region, an old mountain man asked the younger upstart, "Well pilgrim, was it worth the trouble?" to which Johnson responded, "Huh, what trouble?" Tuttle's journey with John Wimber, the Vineyard, and his family will make you chuckle and cry at the same time. I think I know the answer to, "Well Carl, was it worth the trouble?"

Phil Strout, National Director of Vineyard USA

Reading Reckless Mercy provides the reader an insider's perspective of how John Wimber mentored leaders, in particular, one leader—Carl Tuttle. John's methods were not perfect, but they did challenge and empower a whole generation of Jesus followers to become committed disciples who "did the stuff that Jesus did." This book is engaging, informative, humorous, and heartbreaking all at the same time. In the end, the book is a story about redemption. Reckless Mercy is not just something we receive from God; it is something we can give to each other.

Charles Bello, author of *Prayer as a Place*, church planter, and pastor

All great leaders walk with a limp. The Holy Spirit birthed a worldwide church movement called the Vineyard. Read the most poignant story by one of the founders and limping leaders of that movement. *Reckless Mercy* is a tale of the pressures of leadership that can generate failure and brokenness. It is also the most amazing record of God's redemption and mercy in response.

Dr. Jason Clark, Senior and Founding Pastor of Sutton Vineyard Church and Doctor of Ministry Program Lead Mentor at Portland Seminary

ACKNOWLEDGEMENTS

Jennifer Miskov, thank you so much for helping me outline my initial thoughts on this book. You gave me a structure to work from that would eventually become *Reckless Mercy*.

Brian Blount, I've dreamt of creating this book for a long time. Thank you for turning that dream into a reality. I am grateful for your hard work, creativity, and ability to make this vision come alive.

Jeanine Blount, thank you for helping me process my thoughts into words that flow so well on paper. I am grateful for your hard work, patience, and dedication in the processing, writing, and editing of this manuscript.

Caitlin Scudder, thank you for your diligent, thorough reading of this manuscript, your helpful suggestions, and the pieces you've written.

Carol Wolrich and Rick Adams, thank you for reading this manuscript and offering editing help and constructive comments. I appreciate you both greatly.

TABLE OF CONTENTS

FOREWORD 1

INTRODUCTION 5

THE SCREAM HEARD ROUND THE WORLD 9

STRANGELY WARMED 15

ACCIDENTAL REVIVAL 31

VINEYARD BEGINNINGS 41

WORSHIP LEADER 59

JOHN WIMBER 79

BECOMING A PASTOR 97

RETURN TO ANAHEIM 117

EXILE 137

RETURN TO VINEYARD FAMILY 159

AFTERWORD 177

FOREWORD

The first time I met Carl, he was an eleven year old tagging along with his sister, Candy, who was a new convert and a close friend of mine. Carl was not like the other young people, and I never thought of him as a youth. He was more like a small adult with a huge hunger for God. John and I loved him right away, and because of that, we became sort of temporary parents.

As time went on, Carl was just always with us, and we simply expected him to act like us. I know we expected more from him in the area of "walking worthy of your calling" (Ephesians 4:1) than we did from our own young teenage children, and that attitude could not have been helpful to Carl. I still think of Carl as one of our boys, and I know John did as well. Carl loved John, and John loved Carl.

I remember years ago, when the church was meeting at the warehouse on Cerritos and Carl was the worship leader, he was seated one Sunday in the front row with John. We had been notified by the wife of an insane man that this man was driving to California threatening to kill John. Carl, aware of the threat, had his eye out for any assassin-types. Suddenly, a man across from John stood and reached into his overcoat. Carl, believing this must be the man we had been warned about, leaped up and stood between the man and John. The startled man dropped the handkerchief he had reached for, and we all realized it had been a false alarm. The threat was gone, but it evidenced the love Carl had for John, being willing to even lay down his own life for him. Carl's love and protection toward John was just as strong as John's was toward Carl.

Because we had loved Carl like family, his eventual downfall and resignation from Anaheim Vineyard greatly affected us. However, I had a life-changing vision about four years ago. It altered the way I perceive our walk with God as His children. I was in worship at church with my mind fixed on the Lord when I heard His voice very clearly, "Where are they, Carol?"

I was jolted by the interruption to my worshipping and bewildered by the question. "Who?" I asked in reply.

A Rolodex of images flipped through my mind as the Holy Spirit showed me the faces of men and women who had been with us at one time but weren't anymore. Carl's face was among them. I responded to God, "I don't know where they are, Lord. How would I know? You know where they are."

I sensed God turning something inside my head so that I could see rightly, to see the way He sees. I realized that I had believed that the Christian walk was primarily concerned with our gradual transformation into His image. Therefore, I had viewed the weaknesses and sins of others as being very serious events. I was reminded of Isaiah 55:8 that says, "For my thoughts are not your thoughts, neither are your ways my ways."

God explained to me that the story had never been about us. It has always been about Him, His mercy, and His grace. "Carol, you were surprised when they fell, but I was not surprised. I've got them covered," He said as He transformed my thinking. I realized then that God knew everything that happened beforehand, and He had allowed it to happen.

As I continued to look through the Rolodex of faces who had been lost to us, I heard God say, "Find them! Tell them that I need them in their place for what is coming. I need them to do what I placed in them to do. For the gifts and calling of God are irrevocable."

Carl is family. I am so very grateful for the way God does His perfect work at the perfect time. I am excited for him and the role he has to play in God's plan. This book, *Reckless Mercy*, is God's story of restoring Carl to Himself and the gifts and callings God placed on him years ago. The whole family is rejoicing with Carl as he gets back to doing what he does in the body of Christ!

Carol Wimber (Wong)

INTRODUCTION

"Isn't it funny how day by day nothing changes, but when you look back, everything is different."
C.S. Lewis, Prince Caspian

This is my story.

It's raw and it's real. But it's mine.

Stories are powerful, because they allow us to relive memories through a fresh lens. Moments of pain can suddenly become a powerful turning point on paper. Memories of confusion can be recounted with newfound clarity. Broken shards of a life can be reassembled into a story of love and mercy that needs to be told.

Perspective is a funny thing. Living my story feels very different than writing it down decades later. In the following pages, I get to retell memories of my life with twenty (and even up to fifty) years of perspective. My story does not feel the same as I write it with the ability to look back on time and weigh things accordingly. While I was living it, I sometimes felt abandoned by virtually everyone in my life; but as I write it, I can now see that was never my reality.

As you read the following pages, you'll see that I was a broken little boy who grew up to be a broken man. However, God crashed in with His reckless mercy to fashion those broken pieces into something beautiful. Though I'll never be perfect, I have reached a point where I am at peace with myself and who God has created me to be.

Getting to the place I'm at today was not a smooth or easy journey. It was full of mess— something I ran from for a long time. When I was younger, I didn't want to deal with my "stuff." In some of the earlier memories I share, my first reaction was to minimize my brokenness. I didn't want to deal with my own pain and mess, so I instead chose distractions that would never be fruitful. I formulated excuses and dreamt of escapes that led me nowhere.

At times, I blamed others for being the harsh narrators of my story. When the pages of our lives are unfolding, it's easy to fall victim to the idea that others are the ones forcefully turning them. Sometimes we even have the false perception that we are in control. Yet, as I reflect on the past fifty some-odd years, it is abundantly clear that neither other people nor myself have ever been the ones in control. Turns out, God alone has been writing my story all along.

It is a privilege to be able to share a glimpse of what He has been authoring throughout my life. However, before you read, I ask that you acknowledge three things. First, please consider that this glimpse is just that—only a tiny sliver of the past fifty-two years. While jotting down memories of countless people, I was struck by the importance of writing only what would protect the honor of those involved in my story. Recounting certain details would involve risking the reputation and privacy of certain individuals. Therefore, the holes in this book are intended to be holes. I am aware that many events are not addressed, but I stand by my decision to make God's goodness the focus of this book. Instead of revealing every gory detail, I wanted to highlight where God was working throughout the years. He has given me every reason to focus on Him and tell the world that His love and mercy is more powerful than any memory from my past.

Second, my book places a high emphasis on John Wimber's influence on the Vineyard Movement; therefore, it is essential to make a clear distinction between Vineyard Christian Fellowship and the Vineyard Movement. Kenn Gulliksen is not mentioned throughout this book, but I would be remiss if I did not give him the honor he is due as the founder of Vineyard Christian Fellowship. Gulliksen and Wimber are both key players in the Vineyard's history, but Wimber was the primary leader in the part of the movement I was personally involved in.

Lastly, I pray that Reckless Mercy, written in my raw, candid, transparent style, will not just emphasize the mess in my life but will emphasize how full of grace God really is. As you turn through these pages, may you see His goodness. Through the raw and real, the happy and sad, the victories and the struggles, God has been creating a story that I am humbled to share with you. His loving presence has never left me, and His reckless mercy has never failed me.

THE SCREAM HEARD ROUND THE WORLD

*"God allows us to experience the low points of life in order
to teach us lessons that we could learn in no other way."*
C.S. Lewis, The Problem of Pain

A break. I desperately needed this break. The
anxiety attacks had started two years before, shortly
after I had been appointed to the position of senior
pastor of Anaheim Vineyard, the flagship church of
the Vineyard Movement. The appointment hadn't
come as a surprise to me or anyone else. Panic had
slowly grown as I had seen the inevitable
approaching. Replacing John Wimber was a no-win
situation for me. There's no way I could compare to
him, but I was too insecure to turn it down. Too much
of my own identity was tied into it to let it go.

To top it off, my marriage was in a tenuous
position. Up to that point, my wife Sonja and I had
weathered the strains of pastoring and raising six
kids by barely keeping our noses above the rising
waters. We convinced ourselves that the added
pressure of the senior pastor position would
somehow make us closer. I deceived myself into
believing that this position was somehow a sign of
God's approval of me, with all my hiddenness and
depravity included. In the midst of all the shards of
myself that were crumbling under the pressure of

this position, I failed to perceive God's mercy extended toward me to give me grace.

After two years of persevering through the mounting stress, I was succumbing under the weight of the lofty expectations I had placed upon myself, a masked persona that was larger than life, and the shadow of my monumental predecessor. I desperately needed a break. Sonja and I decided to take the summer of 1997 off so that we could heal, continue to meet with our counselor, and jump back into the full swing of ministry in a couple of months. A summer spent relaxing in Palm Springs with our children seemed the perfect remedy our family needed. We already had a mini-vacation planned to England in early summer, and Sonja and I were eager to take advantage of that opportunity.

During our time in the United Kingdom, we stayed at the home of our friends, Marwan and Sue. The ups and downs of international travel only highlighted the tangible tensions mounting between Sonja and me. I have always struggled with jetlag when flying overseas, and my untimely naps were wearing on her patience. My response to her was more wearisome than the jetlag. In my tiredness, I fell back upon my standby behaviors toward Sonja— nagging and badgering. I talked down to her relentlessly. She had become numb to my boorish behavior, and the unloading of my pressure onto her was so deceptively relieving that I couldn't stop myself.

I didn't leave the badgering behind me on the shores of England. I threw it in Sonja's face all the way across the Atlantic. We managed to make it as far as a layover in Minneapolis before Sonja finally snapped under the pressure of my merciless indignation toward her. We were scurrying through the terminal to our connecting flight, accompanied by the sounds of intercom announcements and my unyielding fault-finding. Hounded by my constant belittling language, she swiftly dodged and ditched her way into the refuge of a nearby kitchen.

Suddenly panicked over her retreat and reeling from the loss of my victim upon whom I could spew my vitriolic disdain, I lunged after her and grabbed her purse to yank her back into my unfinished barrage.

Sonja let out a scream.

A frightful scream.

It was a twenty-year-old scream, filled with all the anguish that only decades of contempt can forge. It was a scream of protest against the years of verbal, mental, and spiritual abuse to which I had subjected her.

The scream resonated throughout the airport, and it percussed around the world.

My secret was out. The reality of all of who I was had been exposed. There was no turning back.

No covering this up. No stuffing this scream back into her with my persuasive words that had always worked in the past.

Authorities came. They separated us. They put her on a plane home. They set me down to wait for a later flight where I would be more likely to behave myself.

Terror rippled through me. I suddenly saw before myself the excruciating terminus of all the years of manipulating Sonja and hiding behind ministry and secrets. All the years of skirting issues and twisting realities and lying to myself were yanked away, and I was presented with a new reality in which it was no longer possible to deceive myself or the world. I no longer had a partner in the dance of my manipulation to bear the brunt of my shame. All I had was my own brokenness and the realization that Sonja would arrive in the summer sun of California hours before me to spill out the rest of that scream on everyone who mattered to me. I had lost all the control I had spent years clinging to with desperation.

When I arrived at our home, Sonja was gone. The children were gone. I knew she would have escaped to John and Carol Wimber's home hours ago. The realization that I had just lost the Wimbers too was another crushing blow to an already defeated man. I was undone.

Sleep escaped me as tears overwhelmed me. My sobs weren't for Sonja or the torment I had inflicted on her. It wasn't for the pain I was putting the church or the Wimbers through. My pain welled up from the more selfish source of self-pity. I knew no remorse or repentance, only the deep loss of the façade I had cherished for years. I was caught, and there was no way to get un-caught. The sorrow of that thought was so weighty that I didn't have the courage to fathom what damage I had done to anyone other than myself.

Not only were my image and reputation crushed, but my primary tool of navigating my own stress—hiding on a large stage—was utterly gone too. I was entirely disoriented and confounded. There was no coming back from this.

Desperate talks with friends and counselors only brought up a more terrifying thought— separation from Sonja. Separation from my comfort, my children, my home, my identity. My fast talking and charismatic smile that had served me so well for so many years lost their power. I'd lost my wife and children, and the next logical conclusion was just as horrific. I had no other choice. I knew I must resign from the church. I had involuntarily lost the most precious thing in my life—my family. Now I needed to voluntarily relinquish the second most precious thing in my life—the Vineyard.

STRANGELY WARMED

"About a quarter before nine, while he was describing the change which God works in the heart through faith in Christ, I felt my heart strangely warmed. I felt I did trust in Christ, Christ alone, for salvation; and an assurance was given me that He had taken away my sins, even mine, and saved me from the law of sin and death."
John Wesley, Journal of John Wesley

I was born the fifth child in a struggling family in 1953. I grew up in Southern California, largely under the care of my four older sisters. My earliest memories of my mom revolved around the rare opportunities to see her between her double-shifts as a waitress. My father was gregarious and charming when he wasn't drunk. When inebriated, his jovial nature turned violent faster than my young heart could understand. I always loved him, and I even felt sorry for him despite his volatility. He had been an orphan himself and had no tools for navigating marriage and a growing family. Though I loved him, I also felt safer when he wasn't around, because I never knew which version of Dad I would get.

Having little supervision, I often fended for myself as a young child. I knew my mother cared for me, but her frequent absence left me vulnerable and insecure. My sisters soon became old enough to spend more time with their friends or boyfriends than looking after me. Loneliness was normal; it was a welcomed silent emotion lingering between eruptions of anger, grief, or fear.

At age five, we were living in a small two-bedroom house on La Placentia Street in San Clemente. One morning, I woke up early as my mother slept on her hide-a-bed in the living room before she had to start her next shift. I cautiously stepped outside the front door into the early hours of the unpredictable day. All my senses seemed heightened in that moment. The carport towered over me. A misty rain had just lifted, and the scent of sprinkles on dirt lingered. The large field behind our short fence bristled under a soft breeze. To my left, a honeysuckle climbed and released its fragrance to the rising sun.

A comforting, reassuring warmth settled over my whole being and deep into my troubled soul. I sensed something I had never known before. *This is God*, I somehow understood.

I turned back into the house and woke my mother. My five-year-old vocabulary was inadequate to describe that holy experience, but I tried my best to put it into words. I'm not sure exactly what I said to her, but whatever I depicted compelled her to reply, "That means you will become a priest."

I had attended catechism before, and I had been around priests, but this experience transcended any experience of church. It had been God himself. I was certain of it. My heart had been strangely warmed. It was a moment I have never forgotten, and it has comforted me throughout the decades since.

Within the next few years, my parents divorced, and my sisters bristled under the volatility of our environment. I don't have a single memory of sharing a family meal together. Warm holiday celebrations are not among my recollections of childhood. Our one attempt at celebrating with a scraggly aluminum Christmas tree ended in disaster. My sisters may have other remembrances, but I find I am missing memories they easily recall.

Trauma was normal in my childhood, which is to what I attribute my many blackouts of time during those years. Every door and wall in our house was decorated with a fist-shaped hole. I witnessed a neighbor boy being molested. A father sadistically beat his defenseless daughter in front of my eyes. The hours and days spent alone left me vulnerable to see and experience things sexually that a boy should never understand. School offered little protection since I only attended when I had to. I didn't understand school or why I was supposed to be there.

One Friday when I was eleven years old, my oldest sister Candy, who had escaped the chaos of our home a few weeks before, invited me to spend the weekend with her. I welcomed the rare opportunity to get off our street for a while. Saturday morning, we hopped in the car and headed to a picnic—whatever a picnic was. I had never been to a park before, so it sounded fun.

Greetings showered my sister and me as we arrived at this Sunday School picnic from the Yorba Linda Friends Church, a Quaker church. I didn't know what a Quaker was, and I'm not even sure I knew what Sunday School was. But it was clear all these people knew and loved Candy. I was just a street rat who felt terribly misplaced, and I had never been around smiling people who didn't also have a dark agenda. But they seemed sincere enough. People waved. They laughed. "Hi, Candy! Oh, you must be Carl! So glad to see you!" I was befuddled. I was not comfortable at all with this group of people.

Candy introduced me to her friend Carol Wimber, who then introduced me to a boy my age named Bruce Heying. Bruce was a nerdy kid who came up short in my estimation. *There's no way Bruce could survive an afternoon on my street*, I thought to myself.

An excited voice bellowed that we would soon begin an egg-toss competition. Cheers erupted as teams quickly formed. The Olympic Games couldn't have been more enthralling to these bizarre people. I was involuntarily paired with Bruce as I awkwardly joined these silly people in their silly egg game. One by one, competitors were eliminated, and Bruce and I remained in the lead. I launched the game-winning egg toss toward Bruce. As he reached his scrawny arms out to catch the flying egg, he tripped and thudded to the ground. Egg splashed all over him, sending him to sobs. I had broken the nerd! I'm sure I didn't hide my disapproval as I rolled my eyes and shook my head in bewilderment at these very odd people.

Strange though they were, I was also incredibly drawn to their warmth. It was a warmth that resonated with the warmth I had experienced six years earlier that 1959 dawn.

The next morning, Candy dragged me to church with her. The only shirt I owned was a beer tee-shirt—Hamm's, The Breakfast of Champions! Candy decided that it wasn't appropriate for church, so she rummaged through her closet and located a white blouse I could put on over the tee-shirt. Unfortunately, the light blouse wasn't thick enough to cover the beer logo, so not only did I look like a girl, but my true self continued to shine through the costume.

I joined the eleven-year-old Sunday School class alongside five or six other Bruce Heyings. My beer-blouse top and ratty jeans were an odd juxtaposition to their pressed slacks and ties. The class was taught by a three-fingered man named Mack McKinney. When he shook my hand, he nubbed me, and it really freaked me out. Another young man, Howard Parker assisted the class. The windowless cinderblock room looked exactly like a prison cell to me. The other kids recited memorized scriptures and used strange words. That Sunday's new memory verse was 1 John 5:11: "And this is the record, that God hath given to us eternal life, and this life is in His Son" (JKV). Sometime later I would also memorize the following verse: "Whoever has the Son has life; whoever does not have the Son of God does not have life." These two verses remain dear to me to this day.

When Sunday School dismissed, I escaped prison to join my sister in the sanctuary for the worship service. A man named Danny Roach led the singing. The seamless interweaving of songs with piano, transitioning to new songs, was alluringly beautiful. With closed eyes and open hearts the people sang lyrics I didn't understand—"Nothing but the Blood" and "Beulah Land"—with warmth that alarmed me.

It was all too much—the sincerity, the tenderness, the songs, the friendship toward one another. It troubled me, and I didn't trust it.

At one point, I became so uncomfortable that nervous laughter escaped my lips. I tried to hide it, which only made me laugh more. I was embarrassed for these people if they wouldn't be embarrassed for themselves. I didn't trust these strange words and open hearts, and I wasn't about to succumb to their madness.

A freckle-faced, redheaded man looked at me from across the aisle as I laughed. His tilted head, slight grin, and twinkle in his eye gave me the impression that he understood my bewilderment and had at one time been personally familiar with it. I later learned his name was John Wimber. John saw right through me. The warmth from this man stilled my laughter and disarmed my broken heart.

After church, a college and career group gathered for lunch at my sister's apartment. Lunch was followed by a game of football on the street. Football was followed by a return to church for the evening service. I couldn't believe how much these people loved church. I had gone from being a boy who did his best to ditch the rare visits to mass to one who attended four church events in a single day. Candy dropped me off at home and offered to take me back to church the following week.

As I lay in my bed that night, once again I felt that strange, comforting warmth permeate through the layer of toughness I had built up to protect myself. I had known this warmth as a five year old, and it now invaded my hardened eleven-year-old heart. I remembered the verse from earlier in the day: "God has given us eternal life, and this life is in His Son."

Lying in that bed, I asked God to take my life. It worked, and it has messed with my life ever since. I was safe. I was at home. I had a Father, and I had a family.

My life transformed overnight. I stopped ditching school and went to church every time my sister could make the drive to pick me up. A smile reflected the joy bubbling up inside. I cherished the Bible that Howard Parker, my Sunday School teacher, had given me. My mom so significantly noticed the transformation in me that she sold our house in Santa Ana, packed us up, and moved to Yorba Linda so I could be near the church. She never stepped foot inside that church and never had a nice word to say about it, but she altered everything in her life so I could be a part of it. For that, I will always be indebted to her.

From that time forward, the church became my family. Ancient church father Cyprian is quoted as saying, "He cannot have God as his Father who does not have the church for his Mother." Even though it wasn't perfect, that church became the nurturer and caretaker I had never had. And I flourished under her care.

A new school came with the move to Yorba Linda. I stuck out like a sore thumb during that last semester at Richard Nixon Elementary School. I looked different than everyone else in my misplaced clothes and long hair. Not only did I look weird, but I was also gaining a reputation as a radicalized Christian. I became an easy target for bullies.

Some boys wanted to fight me, but I said I couldn't. "Why?" they asked. "What do you mean you can't fight?"

"Because Jesus said to turn the other cheek," I replied. "If you want to hit me, hit me. But I won't hit back."

They walked away.

Not only did I continue to grow in my own faith, but my faith was contagious to kids around me. I was developing as a natural leader. I read the Word of God voraciously, and I shared everything I learned with everyone who would listen. By the time I started seventh grade, I was leading a Bible study with thirty to forty other students in my junior high school.

Along with those who admired me came those who mocked me. I acquired the moniker "Brother Carl" and was relentlessly harassed for my beliefs. Over the next year, my resolve slowly crumbled under the familiar resound of criticism. I started to believe once again how worthless I was and that not even God cared about me.

On the last day of school in seventh grade, I cleaned out my locker. Buried beneath months of school papers and notebooks I found the Bible Howard Parker had given me over a year earlier. Anger rose up in me, and I tossed the Bible into the garbage along with my papers. I turned my back on that trashcan and anything having to do with God.

With the summer heat came summer friends. Goodbye to nerdy churchgoers and hello to trouble. Alcohol and pot soon became my companions as well; they helped me regain a sense of control over my life. Summer turned to fall as my resolve to remain in control grew. My rare appearances at church through eighth grade couldn't make a dent in the tough exterior I was building to once again protect myself.

One evening in the early fall of my ninth grade year, I was caught in a dilemma. A friend had found some acid and given it to me to sell. It seemed like a good opportunity to earn a little extra cash, but I convinced myself I needed to try the product before I could sell it. I dropped the acid after school, thinking it would wear off before my busy schedule for the evening began. My heart raced as I found myself on an endless trip. I actually went to church while tripping out. The music pounded in my head as swirling images filled my mind. The high continued as I ambled into Candy's house to fulfill my commitment to babysit her kids that evening. By the time I made it home hours later, I was still tripping. It terrified me. Confused by the acid and unable to calm down from the high, I sought the only clarity and peace of mind I had ever known.

I called out to God. "God, if you get me off this trip, I will turn back to you," I prayed desperately.

Sleep came upon me instantly.

When I finally awoke in the morning, I was drawn to the sight of a Bible on the side table. My mind was refreshingly clear. The terror was gone. Full of thankfulness, I picked up the Bible, flipped through pages, and turned to a random passage. I read 2 Corinthians 6:14: "Do not be yoked together with unbelievers. For what do righteousness and wickedness have in common? Or what fellowship can light have with darkness?" Understanding of what I must do filled my mind and settled into my heart.

I went to each of my friends and told them I had given my life back to the Lord. I could no longer be friends with them despite our close involvement for over a year. I couldn't hang out with them and have what God wanted for me, and I intended to never let go of the life God was offering.

The problem was I didn't know who I should hang out with. I had abandoned any Christian friends I previously had, but I realized I couldn't maintain my commitment to God without forming new Christian friendships. I knew of several kids from Friends Church who went to my school, and I wondered if they would be willing to be my friends. I was still a misfit for their shiny group. Honestly, I didn't even like them at first, but I desperately knew I needed them. I pestered them into letting me hang out with them and manufactured as many reasons as I could imagine to spend as much time as possible with them. Our school had an open campus policy, so I would spend only the first couple of hours in class and the rest of my day was free. Many of those free hours were spent with those friends from church, and they really helped me through that transitional time.

I once again became a regular attender of John Wimber's Tuesday night Bible studies. I regained his trust that had been lost during the year I had avoided him like the plague. I knew he had seen right through me, and my absence had spoken more than any smooth-talking words could offer. Likewise, my reappearance spoke volumes, and John swiftly enfolded me back into his mentorship.

The youth group at the Quaker church soon became a home away from home for me. I experienced the comfort of knowing these other kids and letting them truly know me as well. I could always count on them to welcome me into their lunch crowd in the school cafeteria. However, I eventually gained the strength to trust myself around other students as well. I became well known and respected in a variety of circles: athletes, drama students, artists, and so on. Before long, I wasn't simply attending Christian clubs and Bible studies at school again—I was leading them. Not only did I become a leader at school and youth group, I eventually became the president of all the Friends Church youth groups in our region.

I became known once again at school as Brother Carl, but this time I wore the title with pride. Whatever shame I had experienced before was forged into a badge of honor. I gained a reputation for praying for my classmates and being fluent in conversations about Christ. I was able to lead many fellow students to the Lord and help them become part of our church community. My influence was so trusted that I was eventually asked to speak in a school debate in the lecture hall, facing off against an atheist and an agnostic.

When I wasn't at school, church, or Candy's house, I was incessantly pestering Bob Fulton, my youth pastor. I was very hungry for the Word of God, and I barraged Bob with questions. One day in exasperation, he handed me a Greek word study, a concordance, and a Bible dictionary. "Go look it up for yourself," he dared.

Bob created a monster. Not only did I find answers, but I also unearthed greater inquiries. Before long, I was asking Bob even harder questions. Armed with what I was learning from his tools, I began questioning our church's methodology. "Why don't we baptize people in the Quaker church?" I quipped. "Jesus said to baptize people."

"Can you explain why we don't take communion when it's central to Paul's understanding of the church?"

"Why don't we speak in tongues when it's clearly a gift of the Holy Spirit?"

It's a wonder Bob and I ever maintained a friendship!

John Wimber became my closest mentor during those years. He was undeniably the main influencer in my life, much more so than my peers or Bob or Candy. I was a regular at his Bible studies, and he eventually started handing responsibilities over to me. In typical Wimber style, he never did this subtly. I would show up on a Tuesday night, eager for another Bible study led by John, when he would lean over and say, "Hope you've got something good to share, because you're leading tonight." It was a horrible experience! Those people didn't want to hear from me. Like me, they had come to hear the wisdom of Wimber. No one wanted to listen to a punk kid. On several occasions, I would arrive and he would abandon me, leaving all of us in disappointment. Once he even had me lead a women's group. Who in his right mind would send a teenage boy to lead a women's group? Only the genius of John Wimber could have thought that to be a brilliant idea. John placed me on a quick learning curve where I had to think on my feet, armed only with what God was speaking to me, and for that I was grateful.

By the end of my term in high school, John had taken a job working with C. Peter Wagner on church growth. Without John's protective covering, I wasn't as acceptable in the congregation anymore. A few years of church polish couldn't completely remove the rough edges from this street rat.

That warmth I experienced at age five has remained with me every day of my life since. It chased me into that picnic with strangers. It lingered with the Bible in the trashcan in seventh grade. It wooed me when I was so high I thought I might die. And it protected me as a teen struggling to find my own identity.

I was a worthless ragamuffin who was doomed to a degraded life that couldn't have amounted to anything good. God's mercy swooped down and said, "Stop!" His mercy incites the great exchange. His life overcomes our death. His love overtakes our sin. His mercy took this punk kid, rooted me in a church, formed me under the watchful eye of a loving mentor, and provided me the one thing I desperately needed most of all—a family.

ACCIDENTAL REVIVAL

*"You never have to advertise a fire. Everyone comes
running when there's a fire. Likewise, if your church is on
fire, you will not have to advertise it. The community will
already know it."*
Leonard Ravenhill

After high school, I was ready for a new start.
John Wimber's new position with Wagner had left us
estranged due to the distance of time and space, and I
certainly didn't have any family ties keeping me in
Southern California. Without John present, there
wasn't any reason to stick around.

Several people from our church, including my
friends Doug and Sandy Marts, had moved up to
Portland to be involved in a Friends Church there. It
was a neighborhood church positioned in a
predominantly black area and pastored by Sheldon
Newkirk, former pastor of the Yorba Linda Friends
Church. Portland sounded as good as anywhere else,
so I packed my few belongings and joined what God
was doing up north. I worked with kids there and
helped with the youth group. It was a rewarding way
to spend a couple of years, until I started exchanging
letters with a girl back down in SoCal. I'm fairly
certain it was the lure of a young lady more than
clear direction from God that sent me back to Yorba
Linda in 1974.

Upon arriving home, I jumped right back into the swing of things at Yorba Linda Friends Church. It wasn't long before I started a Bible study for renegades—all the unacceptable kids that liked to smoke and drink too much and looked more like me than church ilk. Not only was I once again attending the Friends Church, I was also leading small groups and teaching a high school Sunday School class there. Unfortunately, I wasn't exactly their flavor of the month. John's absence only accentuated the dissonance between my ratty tennis shoes and their polished leather wing tips. My permitted involvement was predominantly consigned to Sunday nights.

In December of 1975, I was invited to a Christmas party at Dick and Lynn Heying's house. John and Carol were back in the area, and they made an unexpected appearance at the party.

At one point in the evening, John sat down at the piano and started to sing "I'd Rather Have Jesus Than Anything." Eyes lit up around the room as a hush settled. The warmth of his voice began to gently rekindle hope in the burnt-out hearts gathered around the piano.

I knew how to sing in tune. I even knew how to strum a guitar in rhythm. But I didn't know how to do what John did so magically. I sang, but something more happened when John was behind the piano. My heart warmed and felt it would explode. A lump in my throat made breathing difficult. I glimpsed around the room through the tears in my eyes to see John's singing having a similar effect on everyone present. Remembering myself, I suddenly became embarrassed. I felt like that eleven year old again, sitting uncomfortably through my first church service with John staring at me. Too intimate. Too real. It's just not what I did.

But, oh! It's what I wanted to do!

Later that evening, after all the cider and desserts had been consumed and conversations were dying down, I heard a familiar voice. "Hey Carl," chimed John, "Carol and I have this new place in Arrowhead, up in the mountains. You should come spend a weekend with us."

"Sure! I'll come," I replied.

"No, you won't," chuckled John. He knew me better than I knew myself.

John and Carol's invitations kept coming, and I kept declining. Two weeks passed, three weeks, then four. I finally decided I'd go if I could talk my roommate Roger into going with me. We spent all that weekend in the mountains with the Wimbers, and we loved every minute of it. It felt like I was in a family again.

John took us to a nearby church on Sunday, Calvary Chapel Twin Peaks, where we met the pastor, Don McClure. Calvary Chapel was an evangelical fellowship of churches birthed in Southern California during the 1960s during the height of the Jesus Movement. It didn't take long at Calvary Chapel Twin Peaks to determine that Don McClure was a long-winded preacher, so I settled into my seat. Half an hour of unconnected points and scriptures had passed, and I was definitely beginning to question John's opinions on this man. But then the magic happened. In the last ten minutes, I scooted to the edge of my seat. My heart was pierced and my eyes opened to new revelation from the Word of God. I had never heard teaching from the Bible like that.

Between the hospitality of the Wimbers and the preaching at Calvary Chapel Twin Peaks, Roger and I dared not refuse the invitations to return. Once we had tasted Carol's food, especially her amazing salads, there was no way we were missing out again. We ended up spending every weekend during the spring of 1976 driving up to the mountains.

With summertime came summer boredom. Roger and I were hanging out at our place one night after church when we realized how hungry we were. Dissatisfied with anything our bachelor pantry had to offer, I suggested we raid my sister's house to see if she had any better grub. We hopped in the car and drove to Yorba Linda to Candy's place.

When we arrived, we saw a few other cars there. Bob and Penny Fulton were at the house, as was Carol Wimber, my sister and brother-in-law, and maybe one or two others. Our grumbling stomachs led us through the door only to realize we had interrupted a pretty intense conversation.

Over the years, others have recollected this evening a little differently than what I recall, but in my interpretation of the events of that evening, it was clear to me that Carol Wimber was holding court. She was describing a book she had been reading on hunger for God. Every face was riveted toward her, listening intently. As her descriptions of hunger poured out, it resonated with every person in the room. Souls famished for a touch from God. Desperate hearts yearned for more of His presence. Nothing but more of God could quench this hunger. I thought my empty stomach had brought me to Candy's house that night, but it was actually a hunger much deeper that was crying out for more of Jesus. We prayed, we talked, and we wept.

As the evening came to a close, Bob suggested we gather again the following Sunday evening. We didn't know what to do or what to expect, but we all agreed that we weren't going to talk about the Friends Church. This wasn't about a church; this was about a desperate need to encounter God. We would only discuss the things God was stirring in our own hearts and how we could pray for each other.

"Hey Carl," Bob interjected, "bring your guitar next time."

Little did any of us know that within weeks, our little gathering of eight people would grow to over a hundred. My sister's tiny house bulged under the presence of people who crowded every corner, packed every hallway, peered in through every window, and even lurched underneath tables in an attempt to find a seat. My guitar was pressed against my chest and my back fixed to the wall to make room for as many people as possible. Desperation drew this crowd, and it was a hunger only God could satisfy. Weeks became months as the intensity of our hunger only grew.

One particular night, I gently strummed my guitar as 115 souls were gathered by a united need for God. I sang out the simple chorus, "Praise you, Father. Bless you, Jesus. Holy Spirit, thank you for being here." The refrain grew sweeter each time we sang it as our hearts yearned for more of God.

Whoosh! The room filled. This time it was more than the bodies crushed shoulder to shoulder. It was something much more. God filled the room.

Nobody moved. No one shook. No one prayed. No words were uttered to interrupt this somber moment. Not even the sound of a single breath rose from the lips of anyone present there. A holy fear coursed through me. *God* was here! I couldn't even lift my head because it would have been irreverent in such a holy moment.

That was the day singing became worship for me.

As we continued to gather over the following weeks and months, our hunger and desperation grew. Worship changed for us. We noticed that there was a difference between songs we sang about God and songs we sang directly to God. When we sang to God, His presence intensified. Simple love songs to Jesus like "I Love You Lord" and "Father, I Adore You" became the bread we feasted upon.

Our accidental revival continued through that summer and fall of 1976 into the next spring. Yorba Linda Friends Church was not too happy with us. They had heard rumors of a lady in our group who spoke in tongues, and it all seemed a little too charismatic for their evangelical moorings. They had encountered problems with Holy Spirit fanatics in the past, and they weren't afraid to deal with us decisively and definitively.

In an attempt to calm their fears, we invited the leaders of the church to attend one Sunday evening. The pastor, Barney Shaffer, recognized that this was a move of God and was impressed by what we were doing. He became an ardent defender of our meetings, but sadly, he was unable to persuade the other elders of our validity. John and Carol mediated a lot of conversations on our behalf during that time. Eventually, Barney Shaffer would lose his job, presumably over our Sunday night group.

At one point, John and Carol offered to move the meetings from Candy's house to the church in hopes to assuage the church's fears. The church agreed, and we decided we would meet in the fellowship hall. Over one hundred people arrived that evening.

I opened up the meeting, just as I had done every other Sunday evening at Candy's house. Guitar in hand, I began with prayer and a scripture. I had found the perfect scripture to exemplify everything I felt and all the hunger our group had been expressing for months. I read from Revelation 3:17: "You say, 'I am rich; I have acquired wealth and do not need a thing.' But you do not realize that you are wretched, pitiful, poor, blind, and naked." I stood there a wretched man. I could see how naked and poor I was. Without Jesus, I had nothing.

What I didn't realize was that the leaders from the Friends Church also saw my wretchedness. They saw my ratty jeans. They saw my faded tee-shirt. Toes protruded from the worn seams of my scruffy tennis shoes.

I'm pretty sure it was the tennis shoes that put them over the edge. Those second-hand shoes were all I had. I was naked. I was poor. I was pitiful. And they wanted nothing of me, and they wanted nothing to do with our desperate group.

"Maybe you guys should think about starting your own church," they proffered after that evening.

"We can't! We won't!" John and Carol countered.

"Why won't you?"

"We won't go without your blessing," John and Carol insisted.

Some time passed while the Friends Church deliberated our ultimatum. Eventually, and reluctantly, they decided it was best for all of us for them to write us a letter of blessing.

We listened with rapt attention as John read the letter aloud. Apparently, the Holy Spirit had fallen upon this elder as he had written the letter, whether he ever knew it or not. It was an incredible blessing, and we carried that blessing with us. We received it, cherished it, walked in the freedom it offered us, and operated under that blessing from that day on. That blessing ushered the way for us to flourish beyond the bounds of what a house could contain, expand our numbers into the thousands, and birth a movement of worldwide influence.

VINEYARD BEGINNINGS

"As the deer pants for streams of water, so my soul pants
for you, my God. My soul thirsts for God, for the living God.
When can I go and meet with God?"
Psalm 42: 1-2

"Why don't you become a Calvary Chapel?"

Don McClure's suggestion helped clarify the question we had all been asking—*what now*? The Quakers had given us the blessing of strong roots, core values, and the bedrock from which we could build. Now they had also given us the blessing to leave and flourish in a different context. Don McLure's invitation to join Calvary Chapel seemed to be the next step for us. So, one evening in 1977, Don laid hands on John Wimber, Bob Fulton, and myself and ordained us as Calvary Chapel pastors.

My childhood had taught me many coping mechanisms, some helpful, some destructive. I used one that evening—the capacity to hide my own shame from the people around me. As Don laid his hands on me and hundreds of eyes were turned toward me, I bowed my head, not in prayer, but to hide the utter inadequacy that was threatening to show itself in my trembling hands and quavering voice. My head remained down as I slunk back to my seat.

I was a mistake, and no one else seemed to notice. What was I doing standing next to John Wimber and Bob Fulton being ordained as a minister of the gospel? When would everyone realize that one of these things didn't look like the others? I hid my bewilderment and shame by donning my best theological façade, telling myself that God worked in mysterious ways. If John and Don thought this was a good idea, who was I to contradict them?

A couple of weeks later on Mother's Day 1977, our little church had its first official meeting. We didn't have a building to meet in, and we had long outgrown a house gathering. We met in a Masonic lodge on Main Street in Yorba Linda. Ironically, it was directly across the street from the former location of the Friends Church. Our first meeting gathered 130 adults, and we set up a room in the lodge for the children.

I walked into the building that morning under a rain-drenched sky with guitar in hand. I saw John setting up his piano. Dick Heying assembled his drum kit. I pulled out my guitar and started tuning it. *How was this all going to work? Was I supposed to lead the songs? I had always led worship when we met at the house, but this was different. This was a church! Shouldn't John take worship over? He was much more qualified. How in the world did I just become a pastor to these people? Shouldn't the real leaders take over now?* The questions and doubts swirled as the room began to fill.

The clock hand hit ten, and John glanced at me.

"Well," he smirked, "are you going to start or what?"

(Just for the record, the rumors throughout the years of lack of punctuality within the Vineyard are false. There is no such thing as "Vineyard Time.")

I struck the first chord, not even sure what we were going to sing. With every rhythmic strum, the reality sunk in deeper that I was leading worship. I was a leader of this ragamuffin group of hungry people. As confounding as the thought was, it was true. I was a pastor. Unqualified, but I was a pastor nonetheless.

God met me with every strum. It wasn't so much that I grew in confidence. I just knew I needed Jesus. The desperation gnawing inside me was also mirrored in the face of every person gathered in that room. Insecurities, failures, and burnout faded in the presence of the glory of God.

From that Sunday on, I strummed my guitar. I led, John accompanied on piano, and Dick played the drums. Eventually, we added Jerry Davis and Eddie Espinoza. Whenever there was a ladies' part in a song, we would feature Cindy Rethmeier. The stage area was so small that there was no room to add Cindy on the platform. So, we'd squeeze her to the side, offstage. I cringe when I think of what it must have looked like to place Cindy offstage, then make her shuffle her way back to her seat so we could go on to another song.

In those beginning years, we never had a set list. No rehearsals. No words to the congregation. We just gathered, sang songs of worship, and went into ministry time.

Not only were we transitioning from being Quakers to Calvary Chapel, but another transition had slowly and somewhat secretively been taking place during that time. We had been learning more about spiritual gifts and the operation of the Holy Spirit. Carol, who had once been an ardent cessationist, was changing her tune. We all set out on a quest to learn more about the Holy Spirit and engage in these once-forbidden spiritual gifts. During our weekend trips up to the Wimbers' cabin, we would learn more about and practice spiritual gifts. By this time, John and Carol had both spoken in tongues, but I was still fond of my anti-charismatic sentiments. However, I was desperate for Jesus.

One night, I prayed as I laid in bed. Before I knew it, and to my utter shock, I was speaking in tongues. *Oh my goodness! What has happened to me?*

Soon afterward, I found myself seated in the backseat of John's Cadillac on a drive up to the mountains. John and Carol and I were conversing. "Have you spoken in tongues, Carl?" they asked.

Very reluctantly, I ceded, "Yes, I have."

John cranked the window down and bellowed out the window, "Carl speaks in tongues! Carl speaks in tongues!" for all the world to hear. I rolled my eyes and slunk down further into the back seat.

Our curiosity grew as we tenuously stepped out into the unknown territories of spiritual gifts. We would secretly visit a nearby charismatic church to see what they did. We didn't care for the style, but desperately wanted more of the power of God. We slowly began experimenting with operating in spiritual gifts at church, but rather than looking to the charismatic models around us, we leaned heavily upon our Quaker roots to govern our style of delivery.

John wanted ministry time to be more natural, and he wanted to encourage the ministry of the gifts in every believer. He intentionally restrained his own gifts to emphasize the accessibility to everyone in the room. The Quaker value of "the priesthood of all believers" took on our own language of "everyone gets to play." He encouraged all of us to pray with our eyes open so we could see what the Spirit was doing. We transformed into church that values the operation of the Holy Spirit, the priesthood of all believers, and naturally supernatural ministry. These values, forged through our years with the Friends Church and accelerated with our charismatic experiences, would become central to our DNA as a congregation and eventually as a movement.

Our church services became marked by the ministry of the Spirit. We were eager to minister to people. We wanted sick people to be healed, broken people to become whole, and oppressed people to be delivered. A liturgy began to develop in our services. We would sing songs, often starting with several choruses strung together in a medley and speeding up. We were goofy and had fun, but we also really worshipped. The upbeat songs transitioned to more intimate worship to Jesus.

We followed worship with prophetic ministry involving simple prophetic words for the congregation. Our model for prophetic ministry focused on corporate words of edification, comfort, and exhortation. Following prophetic ministry, John would preach. For years to come, we maintained this basic liturgy of worship, prophetic ministry, then preaching that developed on Sundays at Calvary Chapel Yorba Linda.

Songwriting became a hallmark of those early years. John wrote "Spirit Song," which is widely used in hymnals today. I wrote "I Give You All The Honor." Before long we had a couple of albums out, and the distribution they received was astonishing to me. John was continuing to grow in his own influence as a sought-after speaker and consultant on church growth. Soon his repertoire expanded to include spiritual gifts and the kingdom of God. God was showering His blessings on our little Calvary Chapel Yorba Linda church.

I met Sonja during the first year of that church. We married on September 9, 1978. I was twenty-three years old, and she was only nineteen. Neither of us had been raised around a nurturing family environment, and neither of us knew how to engage in healthy relationships. A year later our son, Zachary, was born.

We had a difficult time from the beginning, but church became our distraction. We had tons of friends, groups constantly met in our house, and we found life in those situations. But once the people left, our marriage was just as empty as our house. I would even occasionally withdraw from Sonja into the false intimacy of pornography. It became easier for both of us to throw ourselves even deeper into ministry in the church than face the hollowness at home.

And why wouldn't I seek ministry over my marriage? The ministry prospered. It was fruitful and fun. It fed something inside me. It became my identity. My persona. God was blessing the church and the people in it, and I interpreted that as God's love and favor for me. *God must think I'm pretty cool*, I thought. *He must really approve of me for all this amazing ministry to be happening around me.* God was giving me responsibilities and esteem, so I assumed I was not that far off. And to top it off, my songs were beginning to gain worldwide acclaim. I was receiving fan mail from across the globe. I even convinced myself that my marriage wasn't that big of a problem because God was showing up!

I didn't realize until years later that I was using God's gifts illegally to prop myself up. God's blessings had nothing to do with me. He showered them down simply because that's the kind of God He is. His mercies never cease. And God in His mercy was showering our church with blessing.

I'm not sure how it happened (I am sure very little of it had to do with me), but by 1983 that little church that started with eight desperate people in my sister's living room somehow grew to a congregation of three thousand people in a gymnasium in Anaheim. Eventually, we parted ways with Calvary Chapel and joined a small group of Vineyard churches. As with the Quakers, we once again received a prophetic blessing from Calvary Chapel that would sustain and carry us through future difficulties.

The presence of God saturated every meeting in that gymnasium during the early years of Anaheim Vineyard. By the droves, people desperate for more of God would flock to find a place in the gym. The sprawling gym would quickly be crammed with people standing shoulder to shoulder, never an open seat available. One Sunday, John and Carol and I stood on the balcony that overlooked the parking lot. I was stunned to see that people were stepping out of their cars and running into the gymnasium to get a seat. They were literally running to church!

Every Sunday, from the first strum on my guitar to start the service, the atmosphere in the room was electric. There were no stragglers. The air was thick with anticipation and the manifest glory of God's presence. Not only was He showing up in the services, but He was radically moving in people's lives.

This is unbelievable, I thought to myself every Sunday. I didn't have anything special. I was very limited in my skills as a musician. I liked sticking to my three chords. There wasn't anything I could add to the dynamic happening in that room other than bring my own desperation and worship.

In a way, I'm grateful I didn't have John's musical acumen or Cindy's beautiful voice. The songs I led and wrote were simple. That also made them accessible and transferable. Anybody could play the songs I was playing. Just as we were developing a culture that "everyone gets to play" in ministry, we were also developing a culture of accessibility in worship. A worship music industry like we have today didn't exist in 1980. The songs we were singing were a new sound reflecting the intimacy and power of God being poured out in a little gymnasium in Anaheim. God was pioneering something new through us, and I was awed by the influence we were gaining.

As we grew in gifts, we also matured in the way we did ministry. John encouraged people to just be themselves, especially when giving prophetic words or praying for healing. Rather than adopting some of the charismatic styles of prophecy around us, John taught us to use the language of "I think the Lord is saying" or "I sense the Lord may be doing this tonight." Rather than the "Thus sayeth the Lord" style that was so prevalent at the time, John taught us to take on more of the posture belonging to those who saw through a glass dimly.

Once a prophetic word was delivered, we would leave it to the congregation to weigh its validity. Sometimes people would respond with "Amen" or applause. Other times, a prophetic word was met with stone silence, which became a form of correction in and of itself. It was rare for people to continue to give words with no affirmation, so the silence made room for self-correction and learning. It was very rare for John to publicly correct anyone during those early years. But when he did, it was memorable.

One Sunday after worship, John asked everyone to be still before the Lord. Everyone knew what that meant—we were supposed to be quiet. A short moment later, a voice rose up in the crowd. I recognized that voice. It was my friend Billy. In his characteristically rough style, Billy began to speak out a prophetic word for the congregation.

"I said, 'Let's be still,'" John spoke into the microphone.

Billy continued. His voice bellowed across the auditorium.

"Silence!" John matched Billy's intensity.

Still Billy continued. His boldness—his stupidity—confounded me!

John roared into the microphone, "Let the prophet be silent!"

Still Billy continued. I was stunned that anyone would so blatantly disregard John in that way. John was not one to be ignored. I was mortified for Billy and wondered if it was possible that Billy couldn't hear John over his own voice giving the prophetic word. I honestly have no idea what Billy was saying because I was flushed with embarrassment for him.

A long silence followed.

"I'm sorry, Lord." The hushed voice was coming from John's microphone. "I didn't realize you wanted to speak."

I was astounded! Most pastors would have been declaring their spiritual authority. John instead placed the spiritual authority where it really belonged—on the Holy Spirit who is the administrator of the church. John taught us all that everyone should submit to the authority of the Spirit, especially the pastor. He was quick to repent and quick to acknowledge the Holy Spirit's role as leader of the church, not himself.

John's influence was growing far beyond the bounds of those gymnasium walls. We started doing conferences, and people would flock from around the country. During the conferences, we kept the same liturgy we had developed in our church services. We were modeling a new of way of doing church for a new generation of church leaders.

We would start with worship followed by a few prophetic words spoken from people in the congregation. Even in crowds of three thousand, John would allow complete strangers to partner in the ministry of the Spirit to minister prophetically in the conferences. No rules and no restrictions. Just complete freedom to grow and receive the ministry of the Spirit. On the surface, it could seem irresponsible. But there was a method to John's madness. His philosophy was to let the bush grow first, then trim it. John knew that God was doing something in those growing seasons, and he wasn't going to step in and trim it to death before it ever had a chance to flourish.

In 1984, I received a call inviting me to go to England with John to Westminster Central Hall. The conference would feature John as the main speaker, and I would lead worship. I hated to fly, and I wasn't sure if I was ready to venture out into trans-Atlantic travel. Nonetheless, I agreed to go, and I quickly fell in love with the United Kingdom.

We arrived to find a crowd of people lining the street to get into the meeting. In an age before the internet, these people had never seen us, so I was shocked at the response. John told me he wanted me to only do our own songs. I protested that these people didn't know our songs, and I was already uncomfortable for them. "They came to experience what we do, Carl," John explained. "So let's show them what we do."

I taught twenty to thirty songs that week. My fears were beginning to come to fruition as I overheard complaints of the redundancy of our music during breaks. However, by the end of the week, I was hearing different comments about the overwhelming sense of God's presence and intimacy in our worship. I began to realize that these conferences were just as much about reshaping culture as they were about communicating content. Reshaping culture is difficult and uncomfortable.

During those sessions, I would lead worship, John would teach, then we would have clinic time. John taught how to minister in a naturally supernatural way. He taught us to dial down and avoid forceful or loud language. Recipients of ministry were encouraged to interact and give feedback. It made ministry transferrable and accessible for every believer.

John had brought a lot of teaching products from seminars and conferences we had been conducting in the US for the last few years. This proved to be off-putting to the Brits and validated their concern that we were greedy Americans who just wanted to make bank. John addressed the complaints in one of the sessions. "We aren't here to make money," he said. "We're here to equip you. We brought these products so you could take these teachings back to your home churches to encourage them. If you feel that the teachings are valuable to you but you can't afford them, you are welcome to take them for free. Otherwise, I encourage you to simply pay what you think they are worth." Every piece of product was sold by the end of the week at face value or greater.

In one of the meetings that week, I was startled by a loud shriek coming from the back of the room. A woman's cry rose above the crowd, and it frightened me to my depths. Soon, a ripple of God's presence wafted across the room. Ministry began to bubble up throughout the congregation. I realized God was bringing freedom to these people.

Thirty years later, through the beauty of Facebook, I had the honor of reconnecting with the shrieking woman. She sent me a friend request, which I accepted, even though I didn't know who she was. She quickly responded with a message. "You won't remember me," she began. Then she went on to describe her experience at Westminster Hall.

"I do remember you! You gave me night terrors," I joked in my reply. That day in 1984 she had experienced deliverance from a demon. She had gone on to flourish as a home group leader and active member of her church.

Many people would have questioned John's pastoral wisdom to allow the shrieking woman to interrupt that service decades ago. In the name of keeping all things in order, many people would have removed her and taken her to a safer, quieter space. But John saw no problems with having her in the meeting. In fact, he welcomed it. What I realized was that God was putting in order what had been out of order. John allowed the interruption of our order for God to set things into divine order.

The following year, we were invited to London to do a conference in Wembley Stadium. After worship in one of the sessions, we entered into our time of quietness for people to prophesy as was our custom. One person gave a word. Then another. Then another and another and another. I was perplexed. *What happened to John's admonition that only two to three people prophecy in line with Paul's instructions in 1 Corinthians 14?*

Another person prophesied. Then another. *Had John fallen asleep? Why wasn't he stopping this? After all, we were there to model the way we did church. This was definitely not the way we did it at home.*

Another person prophesied. Then another. Internally, I was appalled at the rudeness of these people and stunned that John wasn't shutting this down. I eventually just sat down on my amp in utter bewilderment.

Around ten people had prophesied when Ann Watson, the widow of David Watson, stood.

"You have been out in the fields," she began to prophesy. "You have come into the place of worship with mud on your boots. You need to take your boots off to worship."

A blanket of corporate repentance fell across the auditorium. Crying, then wailing, rippled across the room. The entire body of believers there was gripped by the Spirit's move of repentance. As sins were being released so were any plans we had made for the service as we continued in an attitude of repentance for a long period of time.

John canned his prepared sermon, leaned over to me and said, "Let's celebrate!" So, we spent the rest of our time that day encountering the Lord through worship.

As John and I walked out of the auditorium together, I was still perplexed by what had happened earlier with the prophetic words. "What was that?" I asked.

"What was what?"

"All those people prophesying. Why did you let so many people prophesy? You never let that many people prophesy."

"I didn't hear lots of people prophesying," John replied. "I heard one."

My eyes widened in stunned silence. *Who does that?* He had been waiting for an actual word from God. He didn't count all the others. He was just waiting for the one. Once again, John had amazed me with his wisdom. Once again, I realized how much I had yet to learn from this man.

Over the next decade, I returned to England with John and on my own, ministering in smaller conferences and churches throughout the UK. I eventually got over my reservations about intercontinental air travel and realized that I truly enjoyed England. I felt like God had given me favor there, and I loved leading pastors' conferences in the UK. I loved the people and the relationships I developed. It was typical for me to teach between twenty and forty hours in one week when I went to England. This trend of traveling to England at least a couple of times a year continued for the next decade.

I had the privilege of returning to England in 2012—my first time since 1997. I visited several Vineyard churches and was shocked to see that I still had favor there. What was even more stunning to experience was that the effects from that 1984 conference were still incredibly tangible. The equipping that had taken place during those clinic sessions had taken root to allow the Vineyard to flourish across the globe.

Over the years and across the globe, I was overcome by God's endless mercies. On the other hand, it wasn't like I had my act all together. Sonja and I continued to struggle, and my coping mechanisms were less than honorable. Nonetheless, He continued to lavish His goodness on me, allowing me to travel and minister across the globe. In the midst of the flurry of activity and excitement of the early years of the Vineyard, God never lost sight of me or ever loosened His grip on this street rat's heart.

WORSHIP LEADER

"God wants us to worship Him. He doesn't need us, for He couldn't be a self-sufficient God and need anything or anybody, but He wants us. When Adam sinned it was not He who cried, 'God, where art Thou?' It was God who cried, 'Adam, where art thou?'"
A. W. Tozer

I never forgot where I came from or how far God had brought me. Many times, I stood in awe recalling how I had unintentionally become a part of this amazing family and movement. God birthed an accidental revival in my sister's living room, brought me under the mentorship of John Wimber, and let me strum my guitar as I watched the Vineyard Movement unfold before my eyes. Just as it seemed to come together almost accidentally, I often felt the same way about my own personal giftings. Unexpectedly, certain talents and abilities started to develop within me.

Even though I know there are no accidents with God, I have sure felt like one over the years. I never would have or could have imagined that I would be known around the world as a songwriter and worship leader. But it's true. Yet another glorious manifestation of God's reckless mercy. I say often, not as an act of humility, but as a simple statement of fact, that there is probably no one who has received more from less than I as it relates to worship. I'm without a doubt a less-than-average guitar player and only a decent singer.

Most of my songs were written by inspiration, not in the thoughtful manner of a wordsmith or with the careful crafting of a tune. Someone asked me recently how long it took me to write "Hosanna." I answered, "How long is the song? However long it is, double that, and you have your answer." My most widely known and used song took me about seven minutes to write. I scribbled it down, picked up my phone to call my dear friend, the late Randy Rigby, and played for him. We recorded it by the end of the month.

Recently, a friend sent me a video of a large crowd in South America, possibly even a million people, welcoming the Pope as they sang "Hosanna." I have found YouTube clips from many nations with crowds of people celebrating and dancing to "Hosanna," which has always been my least favorite of my songs. Through my shock, I've come to be grateful for the reckless mercy of God allowing me to take part at all. It will be part of my legacy and something for my kids and grandkids to enjoy.

So how did this happen? It began in 1978 because I was the only one in our ragtag group who had a guitar and knew a handful of Maranatha songs. Therefore, I was drafted. By that time, I had already led people in singing. Some friends of mine and I would go out to the jetty in Corona Del Mar and sing songs by Ralph Carmichael and others. When the accidental revival started in my sister's home, I was happy to contribute by leading songs.

As our gathering grew, I became uncomfortable as the worship leader. I went out to lunch with John and Carol after church one Sunday and stumbled through a rationalization of why I thought John should replace me. I'd be okay with that decision, I explained. After all, I didn't want to be "that person" who didn't know when to step aside, the one who clung to a ministry as if he owned it. By this time, the church had grown, and there were plenty of people with more skill, talent, and gifts than me. Our congregation had grown to include artists and producers from Maranatha Music, so I had become intimidated and self-conscious.

Within minutes, John and Carol dismissed the idea as ridiculous and let me know they didn't want to hear such objections again. John topped off the conversation by complimenting me on my rhythm playing. End of conversation. I found out later that Carol saw me as a prototype, something that would be duplicated the world over. That was why they so adamantly wanted me to continue as the worship leader.

There must have been a method to John and Carol's madness. John Wimber was a professional musician, so he knew the difference between quality music and amateur imitation. Nonetheless, John rarely, if ever, gave me any instruction or direction as to what to do or how to do it. By leaving me alone and letting me continue in worship, the effect was to make the worship accessible and transferable. It kept it simple.

Carol had a clear vision and understanding where the Vineyard was headed. John believed her and had the same sense of vision. As for me, I was clueless! It would be tempting to say I was in on the master plan all along. But in reality, I had no idea what was happening during those early years. I was often bewildered by John's choices; though in hindsight I can see the genius of them.

To my shame, I never really put in the effort to become much of a worship leader. I had a natural sense for what to do and how to do it. I've fantasized many times what it would have been like if I had taken the time to learn my craft. The problem was that I never saw it as my craft! Many more talented people have seen it that way, and they have put in the effort to learn and grow. Their dedication has moved worship forward. As they have grown, the craft of worship has grown. I often stand in a worship service in awe of how the approach to worship leading has grown and how good it has become.

Early on, John approached me after a service and told me, "You're going to develop a theology of worship. I've got my hands full with this healing thing." At that time, there was very little teaching specifically on worship, especially the emerging worship that we were pioneering. There were no worship conferences, no nights of worship, no worship concerts, no websites, and very few books on the topic. There weren't even many songs that expressed the intimate, personal approach to worship we were growing accustomed to. Heck, there was no CCLI (Christian Copyright Licensing International)!

I didn't know how to develop a theology of worship. I decided to start by looking to Scripture to see what it had to say about worship. I recruited a couple of people to sit down and write out every verse in the Bible that had anything to do with worship. We didn't have PCs in those days, so they had to use a concordance and write every verse out longhand. When they were done, we color-coded the verses according to the descriptions—bowing, dancing, shouting, kneeling, singing, singing in tongues, playing instruments, standing in awe, being still. I really liked that last one, being Quaker and all.

Pretty soon a broad spectrum of activities emerged related to worship that almost all involved some sort of physical movement. This revelation flew in the face of our evangelical perspectives. We had always interpreted these actions as not being literal. We didn't see lifting hands as having anything to do with worship. Yet when we looked up the Hebrew word connected to lifting the hands (*nāśā' kappayim*), it had a physical activity tied to it. The same truth was discovered as we researched many of the words used in the Old Testament in relation to worship.

Even though we were engaging in many of these actions, I was still bothered by some of the weird stuff people did. It was acceptable to make a spectacle of yourself at a sports event. But in worship? At my core, I was still pretty self-conscious and uptight.

Then I came across this in *Strong's Exhaustive Concordance*: *hâlal, haw-lal'*, which means "to make a show, to boast, to be clamorously foolish, and to rave." That definition perfectly described all those people with obnoxious outbursts of worship that I had been secretly judging! But it was clearly in the Bible, and there were over 660 verses that had to do with these expressions of worship. I realized I had been too focused on only one verse: "Let all things be done decently and in order" (1 Corinthians 14:40).

Despite my own very slow metamorphosis, God was actively moving in our worship settings. Even when I was leading a happy-clappy song, some people would respond by standing with their eyes closed, tears streaming down their cheeks as they adored Jesus. It had very little to do with what I was doing. God was moving, and some people responded to His activity by standing, others by kneeling, and others by soaking in God's presence. In those early days, we didn't instruct people how to respond to God; we just let it happen. There was an awareness and consideration of one another—truly corporate worship. The Holy Spirit was the conductor of a beautiful symphony, with the various instruments all playing their complementary parts.

It never turned into a *Star Wars* bar scene. No one ever hijacked the service. Over the years, I've seen my share of outbursts in the name of freedom. The knee-jerk response would be to control the environment rather than pastor the people. Too often we try to pastor and restrain the Holy Spirit instead of redirecting that attention to care to the people.

Worship is all about God. It's about what He desires. Our tastes and preferences can play a role in what that looks like, but it is never to be built solely on our preferences. The focus of worship is connecting with and meeting with God (Psalm 42). Jesus paid a price and made a way for us to enter boldly into the throne room of grace (Hebrews 10).

Some people teach that we have to go through different stages of worship in order to meet with God based on an Old Testament model. I do recognize that when people gather, they aren't always ready to engage in worship. If they got into an argument with their spouse on the way to church, they may not be ready to lift up holy hands. Nonetheless, we don't have to jump through any religious hoops to enter into God's presence. His grace is available to us to be in His presence regardless of our actions or attitudes. Our job as worship leaders is to bring the people into that place where they can engage with the worship that is already happening in the throne room.

There is a lot that we do and call worship that is not worship at all. That kind of worship is an industry that has been monetized to such a great degree it's hard to see the heart of worship. We are best off to "guard [our] heart, for it is the wellspring of life" (Proverbs 4:23) and to "worship in spirit and truth" (John 4:24) and "make it [our] ambition to mind [our] own business" (1 Thessalonians 4:11-12).

There are many gifted worship leaders doing a lot of impressive things in this worship arena. Whether we resonate with their music is inconsequential. In the end, it doesn't matter what you or I think; what matters is what God desires. Only He possesses scales that weigh men's hearts. If you can't relate to "worship concerts," then don't go. If a different style doesn't connect with you, it really doesn't matter. He's not asking for your approval.

However, we are in danger of becoming consumers. Worship can never be a product we consume. Worship consumes us.

Decades ago, when I started really studying worship, I reached a quandary. As I categorized the words describing worship, such as praise, adoration, clapping, and so on, one phrase kept coming up, and it didn't make sense to me in some of its contexts. It was "to bless" or "I will bless."

As I studied the meaning of "to bless," I found that the root meaning is "to kneel." But when I read the text, "I will bless the Lord at all times," the phrase "to kneel" didn't seem to describe what was being said. I began to pray about it and asked the Lord to reveal to me what it meant to bless the Lord.

I wondered if maybe the best way to receive this revelation from God was to get away from my daily routine to fast and pray. In other words, I decided to get religious about it. I thought I needed to take it up a few notches to be sure I got God's attention. Obviously, fasting and praying are good gifts, but like everything else God gives, in our own efforts to manipulate Him, we can usually find a way to turn it into something other than His intended purpose.

As I was considering a prayer and fasting retreat, the phone rang. Sonja told me that my friend, Cory, was on the line and wanted to talk to me. "Carl, I'm at work so I can't talk right now," Cory began, "but I felt the Lord wanted me to tell you to go ahead and do what you've been thinking of doing. Okay, I've got to go. Talk to you later." And he hung up. I was dumbfounded. There was no way to miss the correlation between Cory's phone call and the fact that I had just been considering a time away to seek some insight from God.

I explained the whole situation to my wife and asked her what she thought I should do. She didn't answer me but instead gave me one of those looks that said, "Not even you are that dull!" I got the hint and proceeded to pack a small bag, my Bible, and some yellow legal pads so I could take down dictation from the Lord about what it meant to bless Him. I kissed my newborn son, Zachary, goodbye and headed up into the local mountains to a Calvary Chapel retreat center where we had access. An hour and a half later, around 11:30 a.m., I checked into my room and began to settle in.

The first thing I noticed was my hunger! Other than not eating, I really didn't have much of a plan. Bible and legal pad in hand, I sat and waited. I tried to ponder, but I'm not much of a ponderer.

After a good thirty or forty minutes of attempted pondering, a thought struck me. If I was going to get some sort of revelation, maybe it would come through an angelic visitation! I had never experienced an angelic visitation before, and I wasn't really big into the whole idea, seeing as most people who had visions were scared out of their wits. But it did cross my mind that if God were to send me an angel, I had picked a really lousy spot. The room I was in was very bright and sunny, and there was no way to black out the windows to make it dark. Surely if an angel were going to visit, I'd see him/her/it better if the room were dark. I was new to all this stuff, and by this time I was pretty worked up with the fasting and pondering and all.

A stroke of brilliance hit me. The interior bathroom didn't have windows! I decided to go in the restroom and turn off all the lights so that even if I got a kind of wimpy angel (I didn't really deserve a full-on angelic visitation anyway), I'd still be able to detect its presence. I grabbed a blanket and a pillow, crawled into the bathtub, and proceeded to wait for my visitation and revelation about what it meant to bless God. No need for the legal pad. This was going to be memorable!

Time passed slowly in that dark tub with a blanket and a pillow. I had to fight off sleep, but I remained vigilant. I'm sure it had been another good thirty or forty minutes when I heard a creak and saw a tiny sliver of light disrupting the darkness. The light got brighter and brighter until I saw the outline of a woman in the doorway. I braced myself for the word of revelation from the angel.

Instead, I heard a blood-curdling scream! I realized I was screaming too. Of course *I* screamed in a very manly sort of way—definitely not in a Drew-Barrymore-sees-E.T. kind of way!

The maid suddenly flipped the wall switch, and the room flooded with light. I cowered in the bathtub with my blanket and my pillow, awaiting revelation from on high, and instead I was briskly rebuked for scaring her half to death. "What in the world are you doing in that bathtub?!" she demanded. This particular maid happened to be a student at the local Bible college and was quite curious about what the worship pastor from Calvary Chapel Yorba Linda was doing hiding in the retreat center restroom. I finally mumbled something about seeking the Lord as I pushed past her and started gathering my things.

This whole plan was a complete and total bust. Defeated, I checked out and left for home—but not before stopping to get a pizza to eat on the drive. I walked back through my front door six hours after I'd left. So much for my time away to fast and pray so I could get this special revelation about what it meant to bless God. I trudged into the living room, much to my wife's surprise, and gave her a look that said, "Don't even ask!"

I just wanted to know where Zachary was. Sonja told he was in the bedroom but instructed me not to wake him up because he had just fallen asleep. Quietly, I crept into the room to his crib. I just stood there, gazing at him. I grew up without the love of a father. I have very few memories of him, and only a couple of those are worth having. Now, I was a father for the first time. My heart swelled with love and adoration for my boy.

For the most part, I wasn't comfortable with intimacy or expressing words of affection to my peers, but it was different with this fragile infant. I felt safe with my boy. Against his mother's orders, I couldn't help myself. I picked him up. His body looked tiny against my strong arms. His head nestled into the palm of my hand. A flood of love flowed through my entire body, and I started to tremble.

Tiny eyes emerged through slits as he gazed up at me. Soft words bubbled out of me. "Zachary, my boy, your daddy's here. Zachary, I love you so much. There are no words to express how much love and joy you bring me. No matter what you do as you grow up, no matter where you go, no matter if you do good or if you do bad, I will always love you. I will always be there for you. You are my son. I love you, and *you bless me!*"

At that very moment, I could picture myself in the arms of my Heavenly Father. Every word I had just uttered to my son was flowing from His mouth to me. My heart was filled with warmth, my veins coursing with liquid love as I heard God say, "Carl, you are my son. I love you. You bless me!" Finally, I received the revelation I had been seeking. But this was so much more, so much deeper than I had expected.

Insights like this are life altering. When we gain insight into the heart and nature of God, it will always affect us in profound ways. The depths of God cannot be fathomed by our minds. We can find neither the height, nor the depth, nor the width of the boundaries of His character, majesty, or nature. But every glimpse we do get, every revelation, increases our understanding that He has the ability to transform us instantly with one encounter.

This was a seminal moment in my life, but it was a single chapter in my journey of discovering God's nature. It was one important layer of the many layers that He has stripped away, revealing the radical nature of God's love. Over the years my friend, Ed Piorek, has taught about the Father's love and has deepened my understanding of it. I continually ask for a "spirit of wisdom and revelation, that I may know Him better" (Ephesians 1:17).

If we get it wrong about God, we get it wrong about everything. If we fail to understand and embrace God's heart toward us, we will find ourselves caught on a treadmill, huffing and puffing. Working harder but getting nowhere. Our image and understanding, or lack thereof, regarding the Father heart of God affects every aspect of our lives. When we fail to embrace God's view of us, we are left to our own devices, and those devices will always lead us down the pathway to religion. We find ourselves in opposition to the gospel, to the "God story" in the Bible.

The gospel is the story in which God initiates and we respond. It's the story in which God makes the ultimate sacrifice and develops a complete and foolproof plan for our salvation and reconciliation with Him. The story says God commended His love toward us, and even though we were in the act of sinning against Him, Christ died for us. The story admonishes us to love God because He first loved us. In this story, we can do nothing to gain His favor, His love, His mercy, His grace, His kindness, His compassion, or His goodness. It's the story in which we believe and are saved—faith plus nothing!

In the parable of the two lost sons (Luke 15:11-32), Jesus gave us a glowing example of Father God, the One who is generous beyond imagination. Two brothers are both lost—one in his badness and one in his goodness. One brother wished his father was dead; the other saw himself as one of his father's slaves. The elder son had an exchange with the father in which he said, "I've spent all these years slaving for you." He didn't see himself as a son, and it totally messed up his understanding of who his father was. As Tim Keller points out in his book *Prodigal God*, both sons got it wrong—one in rebellion and one in obedience—because they were more interested in what they could get from their father than in having a relationship with him. They didn't really understand their father at all. They both wanted what he had, not who he was.

Our theology—our understanding of the Father—plays a critical role in our understanding of worship. A theology of worship stems from our understanding of God. We can attempt to bless Him in our own brokenness, but true worship comes as we understand the heart of the Father and His love for us. We've been pounded week after week with the typical three-part sermon: God is good, you are bad, and you need to try harder. But that's not the gospel. As we grow in our understanding of the gospel story, God's redemptive plan for man, we will find that the whole story, precept after precept, illustrates God's boundless, everlasting love for that which He created.

I'm not suggesting that we can get it perfectly right theologically. What I do know is that there are some things Scripture makes perfectly clear no matter how you get there. For me, one of those things is that the only way to be relieved of our guilt is by faith and by receiving the innocence of the Son. No amount of performance can bring us to the Father. Only the Son can bring us to the Father.

Several years after my encounter with the Lord with Zachary, as we were returning home from church on Sunday, I asked the kids how Sunday School was. Normally this question was met with any number of benign and disinterested responses. But on this particular day, my son, Noah, said it was really good, which extracted my undivided attention.

"What was good about it, Noah?" I asked.

"We talked about the lies the devil tells us."

"Does the devil ever tell you lies?"

He immediately responded with a loud, "Yes!"

"What lies does the devil tell you?" I asked.

"At night, just before I'm ready to fall asleep, the devil tells me that you and Mommy don't love me as much as you love Zachary, Mercy and Sophie." (Carlton and Lucy were yet to arrive on the scene.)

"Oh, Noah, that's a complete and total lie!" I asked if he had received prayer, and he said he had, but we prayed with him again when we got home.

I'm thankful we were part of a church that believed in the Word and the works of God, and that Noah wasn't sitting in a little classroom just passing around smooth stones and talking about how David took out Goliath. I'm certainly not against those types of activities in Sunday School unless it causes us to ignore the reality that nine year olds face serious spiritual warfare that has the ability to affect their view of God's unconditional love for them.

The lie the devil was seeking to tell my son was a clear glimpse into his character. The devil didn't come right out and say, "Your Mommy and Daddy don't love you!" He knew Noah wouldn't buy that. But telling him, "They don't love you as much . . . " could sow serious doubt into Noah's heart and potentially affect his attitudes and behaviors well into adulthood. A child's experiences and mindsets often come to fruition in their adult lives, whether those mindsets are positive or negative. If

Noah had grown up believing that his mother and father didn't love him as much as they loved his siblings, it would have potentially had a negative effect on his lifelong attitudes and behaviors.

I think there are many who wouldn't buy the message that God doesn't love them, but they very well could believe that God doesn't love them as much as He loves Mother Teresa, Billy Graham, or any other famous Christian. The fact is that if we dare to entertain those thoughts, we're in jeopardy of finding ourselves on the treadmill of religion—trying to do things that please God in an effort to gain the favor we already have from Him.

God is worthy of our worship because of who He is and what He has done, not because of anything we can do ourselves. To put it simply, when I worship I am giving love back to God. He loved us first.

I know God will judge the living and the dead. I know that "fear of the Lord is the beginning of wisdom" (Proverbs 9:10). But I also know that "perfect love casts out fear" (1 John 4:18). Through the work of the cross, I have been declared innocent. And my constant prayer is that His love will form and shape me. That His love will influence my thoughts and behavior, my every breath, and that I will not shrink back at His coming. Rather, I will be filled with joy and excitement beyond comprehension. I want to be like the child who, hearing his father pull into the driveway, drops everything to run out bursting with excitement and giggling with joy to meet him. That is the worship He desires: the return of affection from a son or daughter who has already been lavished with love from his or her Father.

JOHN WIMBER

*"If you're thinking of becoming a Christian, I warn you,
you're embarking on something, which will take the whole
of you."*
C.S. Lewis, Mere Christianity

Becoming a father and being enamored with
my own son was instrumental in my understanding
of worship to my heavenly Father. Taking on the role
of a father also contributed to redeeming the
fatherless pain of my childhood. And of course, I
cannot deny that John Wimber's role as a spiritual
father was a vital part of this redemption as well.

My first encounter with John Wimber was in
the summer of 1965 at a Sunday School picnic. It
wasn't an encounter exactly; I simply saw him. He
was standing encircled by some other men who
seemed to be very interested in what he had to say.
He was wearing Bermuda shorts, wraparound
sunglasses, and what looked like a bowling shirt and
house slippers. I would discover later this was his
Sunday night uniform as opposed to a suit without a
tie, which would have been considered casual wear
at the time.

I don't know why, but I was impressed. I
didn't meet him at the time. I just saw him. I guess he
stood out to me as being cool in a sea of uncool
people. I was only eleven, but I was surrounded by

people who were developing their personas and prejudices, including me. At the time, I was mostly interested in becoming a punk.

From that moment on, John became a central figure in my life. In fact, he still is today and will be until the day I die. There was a time I wouldn't have said that during my years of individuation, that time as a young person when you're developing your own identity and resent the influence that others may play. But truth be told, I wouldn't have accomplished anything apart from John Wimber. I know I have my own gifts, talents, and personality, but he gave me a platform to become much more than I could have or would have by myself.

I don't idolize John. I know he was a man. But the fact is he was a unique man who not only had a unique impact on me but also on the worldwide church.

One of the things we all learned from John was to love Christ, His church, and His cause. Those three priorities remain the primary influences in my life today. I have loved Jesus from the age of eleven, and to this day whenever I talk about Him, I get emotional. That's right—I cry!

I can relate so much to the people Jesus was kind to—sinners, marginalized, overlooked, and discounted. I was a child of welfare. My mother worked two jobs all my years in school and was still working at seventy-eight years old.

The night she died, she had dressed for work but was stopped by a terrible headache. She went to a neighboring apartment and asked them to call 911. By the time they arrived, she was gone. She wasn't a person taking advantage of the system, looking for a handout. She was a hard-working woman who accepted the help the government provided to care for my sisters and me.

I'll never forget the shame and embarrassment I would feel at the checkout stand as she made the cashiers aware that she had food stamps, the look of distain that would come on their faces. I'd overhear fellow church members speak of people on welfare with such contempt, all the while knowing I was one of those people.

When Jesus rescued me, interrupted the trajectory of my life, I was as truly grateful then as I am today. I needed saving. I was an angry boy who didn't know how to do life without violence. I tried to escape Jesus, but He has never allowed me to do anything without the knowledge of His presence. Even when I sinned, I knew He was there. But like many church people, I learned to hide it from others. But since then, anytime I've sinned, no enjoyment has come from it. He simply spoiled it!

My simple prayer over the years when I have had the privilege to represent Him to others has been that people would fall in love with Jesus. Loving Jesus makes John's second admonition easier, because it's much harder.

John taught us to love His Church. One of the biggest problems with the church is that it is full of people. The problem arises when these people gather and pretend to be something they are not.

I am aware of all the teaching and philosophies that we have developed proclaiming "that was then, but this is now." I completely understand that we are seated in heaven, where Christ is seated at the right hand of the Father. That's the truth. Of course it's the truth because it's in the Bible. But it's not the whole Bible!

Almost all the Epistles were written to people who are part of the church and yet are admonished to stop engaging in lying, gossip, malicious talk, slander, orgies, drunkenness, selfish ambition, pride, and such. The audience for those letters is people who are seated in heaven in Christ, and yet they have to be told to not engage in such destructive behaviors. The church is not always the safest place, nor is it a place without messiness.

Droves of people have abandoned the church because they have been hurt it, or it doesn't meet their needs, or it is irrelevant to their generation. None of those is legitimate reasons for separating from the church. I get it; I've experienced all those things and then some. But I've never come across anything that would excuse me from being connected to the body of Christ, to forsake the gathering together with the saints. I hear all the time how the church has hurt people. Those who abuse their position and place to take advantage of vulnerable people ought to pay the price. However, I'm referring to more trivial things that separate us, like disagreements in philosophy of ministry, colors of chairs, programs, worship styles, musical preferences, being overlooked, and someone else being chosen. There are forty-two thousand flavors of church available. There must be a place not only that you can fit in, but that you can serve and be a blessing. If you can't be that, then you're right—stay home.

Because I know it's Jesus' church, I look for His nature, character, and essence. If it's not there, then I move on quietly, without complaint, and without sowing division. Just move on.

Loving the church is a challenge, and I'm still working on it and will be as long as I'm alive. I have come to realize that it's none of my business how others do church. I need to concern myself with only two questions. How can I contribute to the assembled? And is there any way I'm hurting the church?

I am so grateful to John and Carol Wimber for encouraging me to love the whole church. Knowing what I think about the church is not the most significant qualifier. What matters is what He thinks.

He loves His whole church, so I need to love what He loves.

The third thing that John taught us is to love Jesus' cause. We can measure the extent we are engaged in His cause by our love and concern for the lost.

I don't exist unto myself. My commitment to Jesus is a commitment to His cause. Joining His mission is not optional, or it certainly wasn't if you came to Christ under John's influence. With John, when you made a decision for Christ, you were joining the army. John would remind us, "You were bought with a price; you aren't your own." John was never a people keeper. It wasn't a crime for him to have expectations of you once you joined. Inside the church or outside the church, your time was no longer your time. Your energy was no longer your energy. Your money was no longer your money. It was all His. That's what John expected, and that's how he lived. I am very grateful for those values John instilled in me and for his life lived out in front of me guided by them.

I didn't always steward those priorities well myself. I mixed commitment to the church with my commitment to Jesus. I threw myself into serving the church rather than serving Him. I served the needs of strangers more than I served the needs of my wife and children. I served my need for approval and my insecurities rather than finding a place of security in

Christ and who He was forming me into. In spite of all that twisted serving, God still showered mercy on me, and He has lavished it recklessly.

I didn't always make the best choices. I was not always on my best behavior. Eugene Peterson wrote a book entitled *A Long Obedience in the Same Direction*. That has not been my story! I can never think of a time in the past fifty-something years that would have been described in that way. Rather, I feel I would best be described by Paul's writing in Romans. "I do not understand what I do. For what I want to do I do not do, but what I hate I do" (Romans 7:15). If I had been the author of Romans and not Paul, the next line would have said, "I'm hosed." But Paul writes and I paraphrase, "Oh the wreck that I am! How will I be saved from this body of sin and its impending death? Praise God I'm not condemned, because I'm hidden in Christ. Have I battled sin? Yes. Have I tried to do the right things? Yes. But nothing has worked outside of the revelation of Jesus and His grace. The grace of God has taught me to say no to ungodliness and worldly pleasure" (my paraphrase of Romans 7:24, 25 and Titus 2:11,12). In other words, you will know if you have been affected by the grace of God if it has enabled you to say no to ungodliness.

My friendship with John is also marked with God's reckless mercy. John told me when I was around thirty years old that he knew I was having problems. He told me that people wanted me to be removed as worship leader. He wouldn't remove me. Why? "Because," John said, "the Lord has told me to keep my hands off you." Reckless? Crazy? Foolish? You judge. And I'm sure some of you will. But I know this—God was and still is having His way with me.

John was nothing if not obedient. I'll never forget the first Sunday night service when John decided to lead the congregation in singing in the Spirit. Some people may think, "Oh, how beautiful!" Well, not me! And not so for many of the Quaker-roots crowd who were present that night. I had brought a young girl named Kathy Jo with me to church that night, and she ran out of the room terrified! Others began scouring The Book, trying to find the code violation or the basis for such a thing.

John was traveling that week, so most of the fallout was directed toward Bob Fulton and me. We really weren't equipped to field or answer the questions. So we were eager to talk to John upon his return and ask him exactly what everyone else had been asking us. *Why had he done such a thing?* He responded with a simple, "I did it because I felt prompted by the Holy Spirit to do it."

That was the only explanation John gave us because it was the only explanation he needed. My sister Candy wrote John a letter expressing her concern. She concluded with a sentiment that put language to what many of us felt at the time. "If you guys decide to light your hair on fire and roll down the aisles, speaking in tongues, I'm just going to close my eyes and worship, because I know God has me here!" That pretty much settled it. We weren't leaving, no matter how crazy things got. Interestingly, many years later, John asked me about Kathy Jo. He asked if she was okay. John was not indifferent; he was just obedient.

John had an ability to wait like no one I have ever seen. The closest person I know today that does that is Mike Pilavachi. He waits patiently and observes what's taking place or not taking place, very much like the model of Wimber. No exhorting, no stirring things up. Whatever's happening is happening. You see it, you bless it, and ask the Lord to do more. As far as I know, such a model didn't exist prior to Wimber.

John wanted the Pentecostal or Charismatic experience, but he wasn't comfortable with the models available to us at that time. John took God's call and gifts very seriously, but he didn't take himself seriously. He was more comfortable in a relaxed atmosphere and strove to deflect the "great man of God" talk, and there was plenty of that. Wimber was brilliant and very gifted, and those gifts were activated. He could have had people lined up around the block waiting for him to pray for them. But very early on Carol had a conversation with him in which she convinced him that he needed to release the ministry to the people. Thus "everyone gets to play" came about.

One of John's keys to success as an equipper is that he intentionally backed off and dumbed it down to make room for others to participate. He would start the conference session and then turn it over to others to do the ministry. Many times, he would just leave! Talk about throwing us into the deep end. It really was a sink or swim situation.

There were numerous times that John would give out scary words of knowledge for healing, like blind eyes and deaf ears. He would call the people up on the stage and then leave us. I got to the point that I anticipated this. All the deaf people in the room were coming up to the stage and I would glare at John. My eyes were silently screaming at him, "You stay right there, John. You got us in this mess. You're staying to make sure it gets cleaned up!"

Another one of John's adjustments to the ministry model was that he taught us to leave our eyes open and dialogue with the person receiving ministry to gauge what was happening. Previous models encouraged you to touch someone on the forehead and say something like, "Be healed in Jesus' name." The person would generally fall over, "slain in the Spirit," and you would move on. No, John would have none of that! We were instructed to pray, speak to the condition, and almost immediately ask them if they felt anything. We stayed with the person and dialogued with them. Talk about intimidating! John's model didn't allow us to tell people to claim their healing and move on. We stayed with the person, prayed more, and didn't give up until something happened or didn't.

Either God did it or He didn't. John taught us to make no excuses for God. We never shifted any blame onto the afflicted person. We just promised to keep praying if they kept coming. Of course, there were times the person was involved in something or had internal struggles that could hinder healing, but we tried not to force it in the moment, not wanting to add to the shame and guilt most people carry.

As for being "slain in the Spirit," it rarely if ever happened in the early days. Someone, probably Carol, observed early on that ministry often ended when a person went down. So we decided to take an alternate strategy. We never developed a catcher team. Our practice was to provide a chair for people who were sensing the weight of the Spirit, and we'd continue to minister to them. It was a "not so fast" response to the ministry that was happening. Many times the Lord was just starting with someone, and they would dodge the ministry by going down. We weren't going to let them off easily if God had begun something He wanted to accomplish. We appreciated the different ministry models available to us and even gleaned from them, but we also knew that we didn't need to follow them if God was leading us in a different way.

In those early years, we primarily ministered in evangelical churches, and they were freaked out by Pentecostalism and the Charismatic movement. John was teaching primarily the same message as the Pentecostals and Charismatics, but the model was more palatable. It gained access where others wouldn't have been invited nor allowed. But John never wavered on the truth that much of the church gets weary of doing the work of the ministry without the power of the Spirit. He was able to gain access to many denominations by bringing the message, "The Holy Spirit wants His church back!"

In an age glorifying the man of God, John was never a one-man show. He frequently travelled with teams, if it be lawful to call them that. These teams were usually one ragtag bunch of teenagers who would sell their cars and do whatever it took to pay their way to be a part of what John was doing. Through them, John affected the church of England nationwide.

I am so honored to have been a part of the worldwide influence John carried. I am overwhelmed with gratitude for all the people I've met over the years at these conferences, the friendships I've gained, and how my life has been enriched. My only regret is I didn't do more. I was invited to Scotland, Germany, and Australia and South Africa twice. I'm the unfortunate one who allowed my fear of travel rule the day. Of course, I threw the church under the bus. I needed to be home to take care of the church. *Bull!* I was a 'fraidy cat, plain and simple.

John was fun and funny. His sense of humor was disarming. We'd get caught in the trap of his humor. He'd tell a story, and we'd all be laughing. Suddenly, he'd lower the boom! You had laughed yourself right into trouble.

I also have a very well-developed inner child lurking right under the surface, which John thought was funny at times. At other times, not so much. Exasperated, he would frequently ask me, "Why do you do the things you do, Carl?!"

I once went on a trip representing John in Honduras (a place you need to take shots to go to, thank you very much!). Everyone was telling me how much they would miss me while I was gone. "I'll be gone, but I won't be gone," I replied cryptically, which elicited some curious looks. The night I left, I arranged for William Pahl, our front desk attendant and part of the maintenance crew, to go through the offices and cubicles and remove all my colleagues' family pictures. I had him replace all of them with pictures of me. I even told him to place one near John's desk so when he opened the shades, there I'd be. He put them in the stalls of the women's bathroom, throughout the halls, and all over the place.

When I got to Miami for a layover, I called into the office to see how things were, hoping to get a reaction to my little prank. I wasn't disappointed. They had planned on acting as if nothing had happened, but I got ahold of a weak link who spilled the beans. I was delighted! I found out later that John approached Sonja and asked, "Why does he do this stuff?" She had no answer.

On one occasion, John cornered me, asking why I did such things. With an impassive face, I replied, "It's because I'm really immature." He pursed his lips, glared at me for several long seconds, and walked away.

While I was a constant source of practical jokes, John was a source of practical wisdom over the years. I quote him or reference what he would do *ad nausium*. But I can't deny how much he's helped me as a pastor. His nuggets remain with me. These are some of my favorites I lean on regularly.

"Feed what you want to flourish." John taught me to give attention to that which you want to grow and flourish. Starve the other things, and they'll disappear.

"Take your time." That was the biggest piece of advice John gave me when I planted the Vineyard Church in Santa Maria in 1984, a time when Vineyard churches were thriving and starting with large numbers of people. It was natural to want to compare growth with other churches. But John was very clear to me that I was to take my time. That piece of advice ended up being a major blessing to us. It helped us withstand marriages breaking up, deaths within key families, and all the other things that require all your attention as a pastor. You're really not counting heads during those times when a pastor is needed for a crisis. You're hanging on for dear life!

Another frequent reminder I heard from John was, "You're not their pastor if you're not their pastor." You may hold the title and the position, but if you have to leverage those, you're really not their pastor. In the thirty-three years I knew John, I don't ever remember him pulling rank, reminding me who he was or that he had authority over me. He did outrank me, and he did have authority over me, but he never had to remind me. With John, authority resided in him. John taught me that if I needed to say, "I'm your pastor," then I was probably not. I recognize there is positional authority, but I'd prefer to carry it rather than announce it. When Peter wrote to the church in Asia Minor, he appealed to them as a fellow elder, not as their spiritual authority. I like that. I know Paul had to pull rank with the Corinthians, but they were being knuckleheads!

John also taught me to "Feed them off your own plate." John was well known for catching people by surprise. It wasn't uncommon for us to be attending a large conference John was doing, and as we were walking back for the evening session after dinner together, he would casually let us know that we were teaching that night! It happened to many people, not just me. The frequent response was panic followed by the person telling John they needed to go retrieve their notes. "You don't need your notes," he replied. "Just feed them off your own plate." What he meant was, we always have something to offer people when we are being fed by God. We can simply share what God has been speaking to us.

It's not that John didn't care about preparation or study, but he wasn't interested in what someone else knew. He was interested in what God had put in you, not what you had learned from other sources. I'll tell you this much though. After the first instance of John pulling this stunt, not many of us hung out with John without carrying our notes on us at all times.

Recently I took a little ministry trip with young adults. I casually let them know they would be ministering to a college age group when we arrived thirty minutes later. They were totally caught off guard, so they asked with some great concern what they should share. "Just feed them off your own plate." John's words came out of my mouth.

I also frequently quote another of John's favorite sayings: "I'm just one beggar telling another beggar where to get bread." John wasn't an apologist for the gospel, but he wasn't apologetic either. He kept it simple, didn't try to convince people, and just shared what he was convinced of—that the gospel is the power of God unto salvation.

John's life and ministry were also marked by humility. Several of us were back in the office at the Cerritos building in Anaheim, and there were a few conversations taking place. I said to Carol, "You know, he's not very prideful."

"Him?" she asked quizzically.

"I didn't say he didn't have an ego! I just said he's not prideful. He won't argue with you if you can demonstrate his error." In fact, if it was something that he did publicly, he'd ask you to remind him later so he could make it right.

At one staff meeting, a man was trying to make a point, and John didn't really think that highly of what the guy was saying and corrected him rather harshly. The man was shut down, and everyone else simply shut up! The next morning, I saw John barging in from the parking lot. I got up and shut my door. I didn't want any of that action. Much to my chagrin, John opened my door and asked me where the man was from the meeting the previous day. I hesitantly answered that he was upstairs. I could only conclude John wasn't finished with him yet. So I followed behind John as he sped up the stairs, kind of like chasing an ambulance.

John walked into the office, approached the man, and fell on his knees. He wrapped his arms around him, weeping, and asked for forgiveness. It was at that point I knew I could follow this guy. He wasn't perfect, and he had his moods. But he was humble and had a tender heart.

I loved John. He was my mentor, dear friend, spiritual father, and so much more. Words are insufficient to express my gratitude to John and to God for bringing him into my life. My thankfulness can only be expressed in finishing the race of faith strong and leaving a legacy of faithful, humble service like John did.

BECOMING A PASTOR

"The authority by which the Christian leader leads is not power but love, not force but example, not coercion but reasoned persuasion. Leaders have power, but power is safe only in the hands of those who humble themselves to serve."
John Stott

As a result of John's influence in my life, I learned to truly love the church. His heart for the bride of Christ planted a seed inside my own heart. For many years, I dreamt of planting a church. I believed it was the most effective type of discipleship that existed, and I longed to step in that direction. John's influence empowered me to start dreaming about spreading my wings and flying with the vision he'd helped birth inside of me.

Maybe it's time to go, I thought to myself. I was starting to get antsy to move outside of John's protection in Anaheim and venture out on my own in ministry. A new undertaking in Oregon seemed like a good place to begin that journey. I was eager to branch out, but I also wanted to be wise about it.

One day as I was walking around my living room praying about a potential church plant in Oregon, I started recalling critiques I had heard over the years from the people around me. I know I had a reputation for being flaky. Nobody wants flaky for a pastor. As I pondered this I came to the conclusion that if so many people I respected carried this opinion, it was probably true. *Moving to Oregon won't change that. I'm still me. I will just move flaky across state lines and take it with me.* So I decided I needed to stay in Anaheim a little longer to work on my shortcomings. I began to learn that life gives you feedback; listen to it. If people are telling you the same thing, it's probably true.

I wasn't oblivious to my struggles. In fact, the juxtaposition of my life next to the Wimbers, Fultons, and others continually reminded me that I had more to learn, more to mature in. I have always tried to deal with my stuff, though not always in the most productive ways or resulting in the healthiest outcomes. When left on my own, my alignment is not good. I always float off center.

I have spent most of my life numbing myself in one way or another because I am simply not comfortable being by myself. Numbing can take a variety of shapes, not just the predictable ones like drugs, alcohol, or pornography. Television, social media, and ministry are all easy traps that keep us occupied and aid us in avoiding the reality of who we are outside of Christ. My numbing often looks more like choosing the busy serving of Martha over sitting and listening at the feet of Jesus.

Nonetheless, by 1983 John could also tell it was time for me to spread my wings and take my first flight out from under his. He approved me to move to Vineyard San Luis Obispo, which was a little shy of four hours north of Anaheim. The pastor there, Bob Crane, needed a new worship leader, and John agreed that it would be a good move for me and Sonja.

San Luis Obispo was beautiful—rolling hills and enormous oak trees. It became one of my favorite places in the world with its brown flowing wheat in summer and lush green hills during spring rivaling Ireland.

The previous worship leader at Vineyard San Luis Obispo had been the incredibly talented Danny Daniels. I would have been an upgrade for most churches. But following Danny Daniels was like Pat Boone replacing Chuck Berry. Danny is a gifted musician and songwriter and a wonderful worship leader.

"You know so much more than you know," John had said before I left. I hadn't known what he meant by that until I arrived at Vineyard San Luis Obispo with my young family. It didn't take long for me to realize that even though I was only hired to be the new worship leader, I knew more about church than I realized. Bob was a great leader, but I had the advantage of two decades under the tutelage of John Wimber. I had underestimated what I had gleaned from that privilege. It took no time at all before I was doing a lot more than leading worship. My years with

Wimber had given me an eye to see through all the inner workings of church mechanics. Before I knew it, my hands were involved in all kinds of ministry. I had started small groups and was gathering people. I knew I was a help to Bob, but I was also becoming a thorn in his side. Bob was an internal processer, and I think my external processing got a little old with him after a while.

I actually really appreciated and enjoyed working with Bob Crane, but within six months of my arrival at San Luis Obispo, the place was getting too crowded for both of us. He called me into his office and asked me how a small group I had started in Santa Maria was going. "Would it be too soon for you to go down there and plant a church in Santa Maria?" He very graciously offered me six month's salary to leave San Luis Obispo and venture out to Santa Maria.

Sonja and I packed up again, this time to Santa Maria, California, about an hour's drive south. Just because we moved there did not mean I was convinced we were capable of starting a church. I was content to simply grow this small Bible study group and see what would happen. We held our first meeting in a home on February 22, 1984 with twelve people.

The Vineyard Movement was flourishing at this time, and all it took to start a church was to hang a sign with the name Vineyard on it, and people would flock to your door. I hoped it would be easy to get this church off the ground, but that expectation also felt like a pressure to achieve something significant. I was John Wimber's protégé, and I had much to live up to.

I knew I had the skills and training to start a church. What I didn't know was if God wanted me to plant one and if this was the church He wanted me to start. I didn't feel like a pastor yet. I wasn't willing to do anything without knowing this was God's plan, not just my brilliant idea.

A trip to Lake Lopez to clear my mind and pray was what I needed. Along the shores of that lake, I sat on a rock and prayed. "Lord, do you want me to plant a church in Santa Maria?" I felt a very strong "yes" in reply.

One yes just wasn't going to cut it for me, so I ventured out again. "God, I don't want to try your patience, but I'm going to ask one more time. Do you want me to plant a church in Santa Maria?" Once again, I sensed a clear "yes" in my spirit. That settled it for me.

John Wimber was an incredible golfer, and I truly enjoyed the times I was able to get back down to Anaheim to play a round with him. On an early morning at Green River Golf Course, we were waiting for the group ahead of us so we could tee off. We had a long-standing golfing rule that we never talked church or business on the green. However, on this day on the tenth tee of Green River Golf Course, John cocked his head and asked, "Are you really going to do this thing?" I knew he was talking about the church plant in Santa Maria.

"Yes, I am," I replied.

"Okay, I'm going to give you three pieces of advice." *Wow! John Wimber was giving me his super-secret church planting advice that no one else gets to hear.* I leaned in to absorb the gems that were about to come out of his mouth.

"When you get home," he began, "I want you to write these down in the front of your Bible so you don't forget them." My head nodded in eager agreement. "The first piece of advice is very important. Take your time."

This is great, I thought to myself. *Take your time. Check!*

"The second piece of advice is very similar to the first one."

What precious nugget would come next? I wondered.

"Take your time."

The gravity of what he was saying was only beginning to sink in when he continued, "And number three is a lot like number two."

"Let me guess . . . "

"You need to take your time."

I headed back to Santa Maria that day with one plan only. I was going to take my time. Because of what the Lord had spoken to me at the lake, I was certain the church was God's plan, but I also strongly heeded God's voice through John's three pieces of advice. Instead of hanging a Vineyard sign and drawing the masses to our fledgling church, I knew we had to go about doing this a different way. I decided we would focus on gathering people, building relationships, and transferring values.

My new mantra became "party with the people!" Rather than polishing a church service and filling pews, we focused all our energies on barbeques, picnics, softball games, fishing, and lots of laughter. Through the course of getting to know each other, I knew we would transfer the values necessary to build the church we wanted. I set aside the conventional tactics for church growth and instead focused on growing people. Rather than investing in a program or a building, I invested in the lives of those God had brought to us.

Throughout the next year, growth was slow and progressive. We officially had our first Sunday morning service on April 21, 1985. By then, we had grown from twelve people to over a hundred. The people were anxious to have a real church with an actual pastor. Partying with the people gave us the advantage of forming close relationships, but it also left ambiguity around my role. "Are you my pastor," someone once asked.

"Well, I don't know yet."

"What do you mean you don't know?"

"We'll find out if I'm actually your pastor the first time I tell you no." I knew it was possible to hold a title and not hold any authority. I'd rather wait until I had the authority to take on the title.

Another frequent question I fended was, "Is this a church yet?"

"Not yet," I'd reply. "We'll know when it's a church, but it's not a church yet."

Church is like soup. You need to have all the right ingredients to make soup, but soup also requires the ingredient of time. It has to simmer. The flavors have to meld to make something together that they couldn't on their own, and that is not a sudden process. Saying we're going to meet on this day and time at this location does not make a church. It's just church ingredients. It's not soup yet. As John was fond of saying, "You don't have a church. You have a crowd."

About two years into our little gathering, now with around 125 partying people, someone again asked me if it was church yet. I looked around, tasted the soup and said, "You know what? I think it's a church now."

Santa Maria proved to be a time of rest and contentment for Sonja and me, largely due to the incredibly close friendships we developed there. Dear friends loved and supported Sonja, and peace settled upon our household. They weren't afraid to confront me, either, when it was appropriate. I didn't involve myself in any forms of acting out or hiding because I didn't have to. I was happy, and so was Sonja. The relationships we developed around us sustained us and helped hold us together during the seven years we were in Santa Maria, and we both flourished under their care. The measure of happiness we experienced in Santa Maria brought a stability we had never had before in our marriage.

But pastoring a church wasn't without its challenges. A few years into Santa Maria, I came to a point that I felt like I had done everything I could do with the church. Maybe it was time to move on and let someone else take the helm. I paused and looked at the church. What I saw discouraged me. I felt like the people were lacking something essential. "I'm not ready to give this to anybody else," I moaned. "I don't want anybody to see this place." As I examined the church with an eye toward handing it over to someone else, I could see that there was a lot that still needed to be done. I realized that all the people looked just like me, complete with insecurity, anxiety, and need.

I had been projecting my own faults on my people. Not only that, but I knew they were emulating me. John had always told me that more is caught than taught. And I didn't like what the people had caught. I realized I had been preaching into what I wanted people to be, not preaching from who I was.

I had not been who they wanted me to be, and they weren't who I wanted them to be either.

"Well this sucks!" I complained back to the Holy Spirit as the gravity of this realization sank in and all of its ramifications seeped deep within me. That settled it for me. I wasn't going anywhere anytime soon.

My connection to the church only strengthened as we began to weather the bumps and trials of life that come through doing community together.

One Saturday evening, I was enjoying dinner with a new couple in my church when we were interrupted by a phone call. A two-year-old girl in our congregation, Hailey Ann Forest, was in the hospital. I had known she had had the flu that week, but I was shocked to hear she had been hospitalized. By the time I rushed to the hospital, she was in a coma.

"What happened?" I asked Kevin and Regina, her parents, with concern. The doctors had run some tests on her brain fluid, and she never woke from the procedure.

I stayed at the hospital and through the next day. In the moments while Hailey's parents would leave the room to get food or make phone calls, I stayed by her side, scared to death. I was terrified by every beep of the monitor. Her heart rate raced to unimaginable numbers. We prayed for her. We sang to her. She was airlifted down to Los Angeles, and I drove her parents the frightening three-hour journey. Eight to ten people from our congregation had made the trip down to be with Kevin and Regina and Hailey Ann. Endless waiting, pacing, and praying ensued. I led the people in faith and intercession, contending for Hailey Ann's life.

Hailey's doctor walked up to me. "May I speak with you, please?" I didn't want to believe the next words. Hailey was brain dead. There was no return from this state. My shock was quickly overrun by a spiraling grief. I didn't have time to indulge myself in grief. I had a job to do. The doctors had informed me that they would be pulling the plug. It was the hospital's call to make, and the doctor had approached me to prepare the parents for the inevitability of Hailey Ann's death.

In one moment, I had been leading a group of people in prayers of faith and intercession. I had been asking them to contend for Hailey's life. In the next moment, I had to tell her parents that there was no hope left other than our eternal hope. Telling them their daughter was brain dead was the hardest thing I had ever done. I watched their expressions of despair, disbelief, and loss swirling together. I held their hands as they absorbed the horrific news.

The next time the doctors approached me was to ask my assistance in gaining the parents' permission to donate Hailey's organs. Again, my own lump of pain choking out my breath had to be pulled into submission as I walked the Forests through this decision. It was the most difficult conversation I had ever had up to that point in my life.

They decided they would donate Hailey's organs if it meant giving life to others. The doctors and nurses unhooked every piece of machinery one at a time except the breathing machine, allowing Kevin and Regina to hold their baby girl for the last time on this earth. All of us gathered around them, and I read a scripture, who knows what. We sang and wept bitterly. Eventually we left the room, allowing the parents to grieve in private.

I still keep a photo of Hailey Ann on my desk. I still weep at the memory of that precious girl. Three decades have passed, but it seems like yesterday. I will never forget the little girl who taught me to be a pastor.

Before that moment, I was good at leading people. But leading people and being their pastor are two different things. Hailey's death forged something deep in my soul and shifted who I am at a fundamental place. From that day forward, I have known what it means to weep with those who weep, to mourn with those who mourn. Without that ability, a pastor is handicapped with only the ability to attempt to say the right things at the right time. Real, honest, gut-wrenching tears speak so much more than we can ever imagine.

Santa Maria also taught me the relationship skills of being a pastor. During one of our barbeque evenings, I noticed a married man and a married woman walking off together to talk. They were away from the group for nearly an hour before they returned. I knew something was awry. I pulled on my standby WWJD—what would John do—to navigate the situation.

I realized John had never called me out on the junk he saw in me. That was the downside of John feeling like the Lord had told him to keep his hands off me. I realized I didn't have any experience to lean on with how to deal with this situation. I only had the guidance of the Holy Spirit, but that would have to be enough.

I talked to the man, and he expressed that nothing had happened, that they just enjoyed each other's company. I believed him, but I didn't let it drop at that. "You are still getting something illegally from your interactions with another man's wife that you are only allowed to get from your own wife. It's just not a good idea!" I was exercising the authority God had imparted to me as the pastor of these people, and I wasn't going to allow the lack of direction I had received early in my marriage to continue that dysfunction into the marriages under my care.

A little later, a similar situation arose with two other couples in our church. I had a sinking feeling that an unhealthy attachment was forming between the two women, and I was concerned they were heading in the wrong direction. I met with them and explained, "I feel like we are in a room with a dimmer switch. The light in the room has been slowly fading more and more, and before long there will be darkness. I'm not accusing anyone of anything, but I'd just like to come into the room and turn the lights up so everything is really clear." Tears and repentance soon followed, and it marked another turn in my pastoral role.

Pastoring is hard work. I constantly fell back on that simple yes I heard from the Lord that day at the lake. This church wasn't my idea. It was His. That yes sustained me through all the ups and downs of planting a church. It sustained me through times of no growth. It sustained me through arguments and disagreements. It sustained me through difficult confrontations. And it sustained me at a little girl's deathbed.

It doesn't matter how many degrees you have, how many theological books you have read, or how many seminars you have attended. None of those other things will sustain you. They won't carry you through the trials. Only a yes from God has the power to do that.

In 1988, a huge shift happened. I had met a man by the name of Jack Deere who had been speaking at a conference in Anaheim. Sometime later

I was hosting a conference with Ken Blue, and Jack phoned me and asked if he could attend the conference with his friend named Mike Bickle. I had never heard of the guy. He was part of a group of people often referred to as the Kansas City Prophets, a group of men who had a reputation for incredible prophetic gifting and accuracy. The four of us ended up hanging out all weekend long. Mike stayed at our house, so we had lots of opportunity to get to know each other well.

I had never met anyone like Mike before. His boundless energy, unbridled passion, and unbelievable stories about prophetic ministry left me in a whirl. I invited twenty or so of my church leaders to my house, and we hung on Mike's every word as he shared tales of his friends John Paul Jackson, Paul Cain, and Bob Jones. I was thoroughly impressed. I had never heard stories like this outside of reading the Bible.

Over the next months, we started inviting them to Vineyard conferences. As we began to share the platform with them, their influence began to spread through the Vineyard. They brought with them an understanding of the holiness of God, fasting, and a life of devotion that manifested itself in a way that was different than what we had been accustomed to. We were impressed not only by their seemingly superior spiritual gifting, but we were also intimidated by their lifestyles. We couldn't live up to that. We were just ordinary guys.

We hosted many of the prophetic folks at the Vineyard Santa Maria over the next few months— Bob Jones, John Paul Jackson, Rick Joyner, Philip Elston, Larry Randolph, and others. Eventually, I invited Paul Cain to come. He had an affinity for Santa Maria and received the invitation gladly. Our church was between one hundred fifty to two hundred people and met in a school cafeteria on Sundays, so we asked our friend Pastor Roger Wheeler if we could use their place for a Friday and Saturday night conference. Pastor Roger was a great friend to us, and the Foursquare denomination always treated us very graciously. I was grateful for our good-standing relationship when I realized that nearly eight hundred people attended the meetings that weekend.

To be honest, the first night wasn't as good as I thought it would be. Paul called me the Saturday morning around 10 a.m. and asked me how I thought it went. I lied. *Real smart*, lying to a prophet!

Actually, I had something else weighing on my mind heavier than how the conference was going. The night before at around 11:30 p.m., Regina, the mother of Hailey Ann, called me to alert me that her husband Kevin was on his way to my house. I asked why, and she said he would let me know. He confessed he had been engaging in affairs, and Regina had found out.

I decided to let Paul know something had happened the night before.

"Domestic?" he asked.

"Yes."

"Is her name Regina?"

The hair on my arms stood to attention as I replied, "Yes."

"What's his name?" Paul asked, which seemed strange to me considering he had already heard Regina's name. I told him the man's name was Kevin, but I didn't share anything else. Paul asked me if I could make sure they would be in the meeting that night. I told him I wasn't certain Kevin would still be alive by that night!

Saturday night came, and the place was packed. Paul did a great job. At one point, he asked if he could do some of the Lord's business. I'm assuming it was a rhetorical question. Paul then called out the name Kevin. A Kevin stood. Paul started to speak to him, but stopped mid-sentence. "You're not the right Kevin." The man returned to his seat, and the right Kevin stood up from his seat on the opposite side of the room from Regina.

"Kevin," Paul continued. "The enemy has a contract out on you. He wants to destroy you. He wants to kill you like he killed your daughter." Paul spoke words of life, exhortation, and admonishment to Kevin. He also told Kevin that God was changing his name to John.

I was on the floor. The holiness of God fell on us and we were digging at the ground trying to find the lowest place to put ourselves. I could hear Sonja wailing out as I realized I was wailing too. There was no point low enough to place ourselves in the presence of such an awareness of God's holiness.

Paul continued. "Kevin, God is going to use you to repair marriages." We couldn't believe what we were hearing, and everyone from our congregation was weeping in confirmation of what God was doing in the lives of this couple we loved so much.

That day in the meeting, Paul called Regina out. "God showed me a Regina upright vacuum cleaner. He says that you are an upright woman." God was working miraculously to intervene in the lives of both of these people, but little did we know that those words would be tested tremendously.

After a few months, Regina was struggling with remaining married to a man who seemed would never change. She had one foot out the door again, and she called me to let me know it was over. She simply couldn't continue in an unfaithful marriage, and no one could blame her.

Suddenly, a thought—a question—came to my mind. I felt reluctant to ask her, but I cared deeply for this couple. "Regina," I asked, "What did Paul say when he called you out?"

"He said I'm an upright woman," she proclaimed with all the pride and indignation she could muster.

"Huh." I paused. "Isn't it amazing that God would say that to you, a woman who has had two abortions and whose first child was born out of wedlock?"

Regina knew what she had to do. That prophetic word that Paul Cain gave in 1989 sustained her through a marriage of continuous betrayal. For the next twenty-five years, John (the name he now goes by) continued to be unfaithful, but Regina stayed with him because she didn't have permission from the Lord to leave. She wasn't a nutcase. She wasn't co-dependent. God had spoken to her through a prophetic word from Paul Cain, and God was the One who divinely enabled her to stay in the marriage.

It took twenty-five years, but eventually God got ahold of John. He was radically saved, and he and Regina have been living on a mission to heal ravaged marriages ever since. They carry the hope of God healing an impossible situation, and that healing started through the prophetic movement. Regina has written a book chronicling their journey entitled *Thirsty Heart: Nourishment for a Dehydrated Soul*. The prophetic movement had an enormous impact on the Vineyard, and John and Regina's marriage is just one example of its profound effects.

RETURN TO ANAHEIM

"It was the best of times, it was the worst of times, it was the age of wisdom, it was the age of foolishness, it was the epoch of belief, it was the epoch of incredulity, it was the season of Light, it was the season of Darkness, it was the spring of hope, it was the winter of despair, we had everything before us, we had nothing before us, we were all going direct to Heaven, we were all going direct the other way—in short, the period was so far like the present period, that some of its noisiest authorities insisted on its being received, for good or for evil, in the superlative degree of comparison only."
Charles Dickens, A Tale of Two Cities

Santa Maria was good to me. I had a good thing going there. The church was doing well, and we had recently bought a new facility. I was overseeing a dozen or so churches in the Santa Maria area, which I thoroughly enjoyed. My family was relationally connected and rooted into that community. But I started noticing a different draw.

In 1989, during the thick of the excitement swirling around the prophetic movement, several of the prophetic voices began sharing with me that they felt I belonged at Anaheim Vineyard. While the Vineyard was better described as a strawberry patch of interconnected churches, their vision was more of a wheel and spokes with Anaheim as the hub. In their estimation, Anaheim was the epicenter and John

Wimber was the apostle, so I needed to be with him in the center of it all. Before long, I was feeling dog piled by all their prophetic direction for me to relocate to Anaheim. I had personally witnessed the power of their prophetic accuracy, so ignoring their input seemed unwise.

To top it off, early one morning, I got a call from Bob Jones. "Carl!" he barked. "Go out to your backyard." Confused, I followed his simple instruction. "Go to the peach tree." *How did he know I had a peach tree in my backyard?* "Grab a switch off that tree, because you're about to get a whoopin'." He went on to tell me that I needed to be in Anaheim and to stop running from God's plans for me. At that point, it seemed not only unwise but downright foolish to continue to delay a move to Anaheim.

As we were in the process of making arrangements for the move, I received a surprise visit from my friend Billy. He shook in my living room as he began to share a dream he had the night before. Through tears he explained he had seen me laying a baby down in the river, but I was supposed to pick the baby back up. He interpreted this to mean I wasn't supposed to leave Santa Maria. It left me perplexed, but this one prophetic dream, vague in its interpretation, seemed to be swallowed up by what I was hearing from the prophets. Bob Jones, John Paul Jackson, and Paul Cain were all putting the squeeze on me about Anaheim. They kept telling me how much John needed me.

As I continued to ponder this and pray, I was reminded again of how much I loved John. I truly did want to be on the ground with him in Anaheim to support him. I felt like I heard clear direction from the Lord. *Set aside my purposes for my own life to serve the purposes of God in John's life.* So, we loaded up our four children and made our way back to Anaheim in 1990.

The time away from John had been fruitful. Soon after my return, John commented, "I sent off a boy, and he became a man." It was good to be back at home in Anaheim and with this man I loved so much who was like a father to me.

The removal of the burden of senior leadership was also refreshing. I was there to serve John, and that posture of service enabled me to be completely honest with him. Whether John realized it or not, he needed people around him who had history and relationship with him and wouldn't take advantage of him. He trusted me, and we were both very helpful to each other during that season.

I was hired as one of many associate pastors and was involved in worship and small groups. I took the groups through a transformation to becoming home fellowships that functioned similarly to small churches. I coordinated the preaching schedule with all the competing voices that wanted time on that so-important stage at Anaheim Vineyard. The church was thriving, my family and I were adjusting well to the move, and John seemed to be in a healthy place.

With the pressure of senior leadership off my shoulders, I was having a blast! I felt like I was walking ten inches off the ground when I arrived. I could do all the stuff without all the responsibility, so it felt like a vacation compared to the grueling work of pastoring a church.

The prophetic movement was continuing to grow and spread its influence throughout the Vineyard during the early 1990s. As time went on, the canyon separating us became more apparent. John was an equipper. From the earliest days of his ministry, he had thrown all his energy into teaching others to do the ministry. People came to church with the expectation that they would be doing ministry. They were trained to heal the sick and offer prophetic words. However, like the slow turn of a massive ship, we began to realize the ministry was being stripped from the hands of the people. They no longer came to church to minister to others. Instead, the allure of church was an expectation for someone from the pulpit to give a prophetic word. The irony of the prophetic movement? The people stopped prophesying.

The contrast between John and the prophets became magnified with time. John's package was a Diet Coke balancing on the pulpit while he said a prayer so simple everyone thought they could do it. The prophets' package was like a bomb exploding on the stage that no one else could detonate. John believed God would do what God would do, and no amount of striving would change that. The prophets fasted and prayed for hours before they felt they could give a prophetic word. John took ministry out of the pulpit and taught people to do the stuff in restaurants, backyards, and workplaces. The prophets only ministered under the anointing, which only happened on stage in an environment of faith and holiness. John had the kind of faith that trusted God to do what God does no matter what atmosphere we were in.

The prophets were so good at doing what they did that we became self-conscious. We allowed the essence of who the Vineyard was to go to the back burner as we tried to become more like the prophets. We instituted three-times daily prayer so we could pray like them. My head started to spin as I realized we were praying together more in a week than we had in the last decade. And it wasn't that we didn't believe in prayer. We just also believed that God shows up no matter how much clay the clay vessel is made up of. Somehow, we forgot those core things that made the Vineyard the Vineyard when the prophets showed up. And it was evidenced by our insecurity and discomfort with who we were.

The prophets were who they were. And they were themselves very well. The problem was the Vineyard stopped being the Vineyard. We let go of a vital piece of ourselves.

By the mid-90s it was becoming clear that the rickety bridge we constructed to span that growing canyon between us was no longer holding up. The differences were too vast. The pain too deep. The square peg could no longer fit in the round hole, and we stopped trying to force it. The prophetic movement went its way while the Vineyard groped around on the ground trying to reassemble the broken pieces and put them back together the way it had been before. We were left fragmented by all the pieces of ourselves we had let go of during those prophetic years.

Not only was the Vineyard struggling with its identity, but so was I personally during those early 1990s. John was wonderful to me, but he was also a father figure. And I didn't have a good track record when it came to fathers. Stress mounted when I was around John because he pushed all the broken father buttons in me. I would realize on a Monday that I was still reeling from a benign comment John had made the previous Tuesday. Colleagues started pointing out to me what was glaringly obvious to them—it wasn't healthy that John's words or actions affected me so strongly.

Within six months of arriving back at Anaheim, I decided to start psychotherapy. I needed to see someone who was outside my orbit, who didn't know me and didn't know John. So, I got a reference from someone on staff for a therapist in Long Beach and called to set an appointment. I arrived at the designated time, got out of my car, and started wandering the facility to find the right office. While I was still a ways off, a man started smiling and waving at me. *How does this guy know me? Is this my counselor?*

"Hi Carl! So glad to meet you in person. The only times I've ever seen you before are when I go to church at Anaheim Vineyard."

Great. Just great.

Nonetheless, I was determined to work on my daddy issues. It was difficult to go through those sessions, and it was even more difficult to leave them and head back to the church. One day as I arrived back at the office, I bumped into John.

"Where have you been?" he gruffed.

"I was seeing a counselor."

"A shrink?"

"Yeah."

"Why?"

I didn't say a word. I just pointed my finger straight at him.

John blanched. "Why?! What did I do?"

"Nothing, John. It's not you. It's me," I replied. "I have to learn how to deal with us, because I respond to you like a father figure. I need to work on that." He was surprisingly understanding, and over the next few years, we did quite well with each other.

My daddy issues were being worked on, but I didn't realize I had another problem that was just as bad—my ego. It didn't take long for my role at Anaheim to grow. I had greater visibility and notoriety, which meant a grander façade to keep up with. I was being swallowed up by this persona I projected when I was around other people. I was compelled to keep that smokescreen on when I was in public. No one knew it was false; they thought it was my gregarious personality. They adored the stage-version of myself, and I enjoyed it too. I encouraged their appreciation. I didn't realize that all that bluster was just my way of trying to cope with me not being comfortable with what I had become.

I had started at Anaheim as an associate, rather low on the totem pole. But within a year, Todd Hunter and Jack Deere had resigned. I became second in command behind John, hopscotching a few people along the way. I was John's right-hand man by the time we moved into our new building in 1991.

I knew I was the heir apparent, and the sick thing is that I allowed that to feed something in me. It was the part of me that needed to become something important; the part of me that wasn't happy just being who I was. It felt good to be so necessary.

At the same time, I wasn't fixated on position. I even made an attempt to leave Anaheim in 1993. But as I discussed the opportunity with John, he gave me a somber warning. "If you leave Anaheim, you will be leaving your inheritance." It was sobering in its honesty, but it also appealed to me on some unhealthy levels. God was affirming me, but I twisted that divine affirmation to feed myself.

All of this blustery self-aggrandizement blinded me to my own shortcomings. I loved the stage, but when I came off, the emptiness sent me clamoring for comfort, often in unhealthy ways. Alcohol was a pseudo-consolation I indulged myself in. I continued to episodically appease my shame with the false intimacy of pornography. When I was unsuccessful at controlling my own self-hating thoughts, I'd redirect to abusive control over Sonja. I am ashamed of all the times I lashed out at her with anger that was really directed toward my own inadequacies.

I was delusional. I believed that all the affirmation I received for my public persona was God's affirmation of my secret self. It was not. I took His loving encouragements and used them to prop myself up and excuse my inexcusable behaviors. I deluded myself into believing that God's activity through me was an indicator that He was blind toward my real self. I forgot just how good He is. He's so good that He will use even someone as screwed up as I was to minister His love.

Each time I acted out, an overflow of great remorse, shame, and guilt threatened to swallow me. I would confess to God, sometimes even to another person. "I promise I won't do that ever again." And I meant it. The shame gave me just enough strength to pull myself together. I'd go on with life, often with long stretches of time when I would do well. It seemed like God was giving me a pass on my sin, as evidenced by all the wonderful ministry happening around and through me. But as the pressure slowly accumulated again over months and months, I would fall back into the same traps. A late night bottle of Merlot to myself. Scornful words tossed out haphazardly to Sonja as if they were innocuous.

It was so much easier to wrap myself into the workings of the church machine than spend time with my own family. My six children required a lot of attention, but my childhood had not prepared me for healthy family life. Our two youngest children were born in Anaheim, the fifth child requiring heart surgery when he was only eight days old. Several of my kids were reaching their teen years and wanted to spend more time with their friends, and we struggled with knowing how to do family well.

We enjoyed camping on the weekends, and we ate out a lot. Other than that, we really didn't know what to do with each other. A friend once suggested we try family game night. I scoffed at the suggestion. The right combination of board games didn't output a magical ingredient that would make family suddenly work for us. Nonetheless, the children developed lifelong friendships at Anaheim. There were plenty of activities for them to enjoy, and the more activities they were involved in the less guilty I felt about not being available to them. Regardless of my own struggles, overall the children still remember Anaheim as being good times for them.

Another blow came in 1993 with John's diagnosis of cancer. He had been balancing the Association of Vineyard Churches, Anaheim Vineyard, Vineyard Music Group, and a million other plates, and many of those responsibilities had to take second place to doctor visits, hospitals, and radiation therapy. It wasn't long before I was, in effect, leading the church. The radiation put the cancer in remission, but it also took a huge toll on John's body. His frame was weaker, and John was dependent upon a bottle of what he called "pig saliva" to moisturize his mouth from the destructive effects of radiation on his salivary glands.

As John slowly regained strength, he noticed how well the church had been running in his absence. There were clear signs that the people were following my lead, and John's simple suggestion was to not change it. John retained the Senior Pastor title, but I handled much of the daily workings of the church.

John and I were sitting together at church one Sunday in November of 1994 when he leaned over to me. "It's time," he said.

"Time for what?" I asked, confused by the seemingly misplaced comment.

"It's time for you to take the senior pastor position." It was like a bomb dropped in my lap. I couldn't imagine a reality in which John was still around but not senior pastor of that church. *Me? Could I really be the person to take this on?* It made sense, but it was also immense news to swallow. As John and I continued to talk about it over the next months, he confided in me that God had spoken to him fifty-four distinct times that I was to take over the church. Discussions with Sonja also brought us to the same conclusion. We both knew our marriage was struggling, but church was a place where we both found life. Maybe the senior leadership role was exactly what our marriage needed to get us out of this slump.

I continued to operate the church behind the scenes over the next year with John as the named senior pastor, and the church was thriving. I headed up an endeavor to collect a compassion offering for the poor. When we counted all the money at the end of that Benevolence Sunday, I shared with John that we had raised over $800,000 in one offering. He was stunned. "Carl, this shows you! They responded to you. This was your vision, your direction. It's your church now." I felt good about it too. It was time. In December of 1995, to a packed house of over three thousand people, I was commissioned as the Senior Pastor of Anaheim Vineyard Church.

Professionally, I was doing well. We expected a hit with John's resignation, so we weren't incredibly surprised when attendance dropped nearly twenty percent over the next year. However, our giving only dropped four percent. That told me that the people we lost were mostly the spectators, and we were left with a solid core of people to move this church forward. Small groups were flourishing. Our staff was working well together, and I was implementing some healthy changes to move us more toward a team leadership structure.

Despite my professional success, I was faltering under the weight of my new role. Almost immediately after my commissioning, I started experiencing panic attacks. Not just a couple panic attacks, over forty of them.

One afternoon, I was enjoying lunch with John, Todd Hunter, and Bob Fulton at Fuskari's Restaurant near the church when I felt a slight spasm in my esophagus. The discomfort in my chest grew as I began to spiral out of control. "I'm having a heart attack!" I told them. They tried talking me down, but the spiral had sucked me down into the irreversible whirlpool of panic. By the time paramedics arrived, I was curled on the floor, convinced I was dying. I peeked up through the fog of anxiety and the flurry of paramedics checking my heart and saw John standing at the dessert cart ordering a piece of cake. Apparently he didn't comprehend the gravity of my situation.

I spent the next hours in the ER, fixated on the likelihood of my imminent death. I was fidgeting with my phone as a doctor walked past my room. "You know, there's no cure for a Type A personality!" he hollered over his shoulder at me. I almost threw the phone at him.

Not long afterward, the familiar pang in my chest accosted me in the middle of the night. Sonja picked up the phone to call our friend, Dr. Ken Wong. Sweat had soaked through my clothes by the time he arrived. Ken patiently tried to coax me out of the panic, but I was having none of it. "But I'm dying!" I insisted.

Ken threw his familiar smirk my way and chuckled, "No, Carl. You're not dying." That short laugh was somehow comforting. Dr. Wong had used that laughter before with me to take the edge off my struggles with ADD, and he was using it again to take the edge off the anxiety.

The panic attacks were coming so regularly that it was apparent I needed to find a way to control them. I was desperate for any kind of relief, and I found it in the form of a prescription for Valium. The panic attacks subsided. I was so relieved that the symptoms were gone that I never even considered that the underlying causes for the panic attacks were all still alive under the surface.

The stress of running the church mounted. How was I going to carry on the legacy of a man whose role I could never fill? John's title pasted onto me didn't mean I could do what John did. We needed $88,000 every week to keep that machine running, and I kept a pulse on our income as closely as I monitored my own pulse during my panic attacks.

By 1996, I was convinced I wasn't going to make it. I started seeking help from my colleagues. Instead of taking my desperation seriously, they would tell me how much they appreciated my transparency. The token "give your burdens to Jesus" prayers were like trying to bail water out of a sinking ship with a spoon. Sure, it was helpful, but a Coast Guard rescue cutter was more in order for the situation than a spoon.

I was also complicit in my isolation. My executive staff occasionally tried to confront me about my anxiety, but I deflected and argued with them. I minimized my problems so that I could maintain the grandiose façade.

To my face, friends offered reassurance for my panic attacks, but behind my back there was talk of secret sin being the cause. If secret sin were the sole cause of panic attacks, then the whole church would be having them. We all carry sin around; some of us are just more aware of it than others. My sin wasn't a secret—it was right there in front for everyone to see. But their speculation was a way for them to rationalize my pain. They couldn't understand that I was simply overwhelmed. I wasn't having an affair. I wasn't a closet alcoholic or drug addict. I was just drowning under the pressure of the weight I was trying to carry.

I tried so hard to fill John's shoes. He had built this colossal mechanism! Anaheim Vineyard was a giant 747 hurling through the air. John had been the only man talented enough to get it off the ground and soaring through the air at forty thousand feet and six hundred miles per hour. Now I was the captain taking over, my only hope being to keep it from crashing. I tried to explain it once to John. "All this activity you see me doing," I began. "It's just me trying to keep this thing going." I didn't realize it was all false activity. None of it was necessary. It was all a swirling mess of my own insecurity. The only person who would take over a church like that from the founder of the movement was someone who was insecure in who they were. I needed the title as affirmation of God's approval for me. But I didn't have the inner fortitude to maintain it.

My marriage was falling apart. I was longing for connection, and instead of turning to Sonja, my thoughts gravitated to other sources. The allure of marital infidelity was a growing temptation. Throughout my ministry, women had always come to me to let me know they were available to me. But for the first time, I was beginning to flirt with the idea. I never acted out on it, but just the idea that I could have an affair was comforting to me. I drew affirmation from knowing I could be with another woman who appreciated me, and this fantasy fed something sick inside of me. I ignored the fact that these women didn't really care about me; I was a means to an end. It wasn't fair to take advantage of women who were simply longing for social influence and were mistakenly looking to me to provide that for them. It wasn't an even playing field, and I was toying with their vulnerabilities to even indulge in imagining a relationship with them.

I would love to say that it was my strength of character that kept me out of another woman's bed. But it wasn't. I was simply too chicken to do it. I was afraid I'd get caught. I tried to figure it out. I fantasized a way to secretly carry out an affair. But I couldn't get my mind around how I could do it without getting caught.

By the time 1997 rolled around, our marriage was in serious trouble. I connected with a well-known and highly regarded counselor, speaker, and author. He agreed to start counseling Sonja and me. Even an expert counselor is only as good as the information you give them to work with, and I was really adept at controlling Sonja and what little I allowed her to talk about with our counselor. I wasn't talking about the occasional porn. I refused to discuss how much I enjoyed the numbing effect of Valium chased by a bottle of wine. I didn't disclose my fits of rage toward Sonja or the emotional abuse she endured. And she wasn't talking either. "Give me another week, Sonja," I would plead in the car on the way to meet our counselor. "I promise I'll tell him everything next week, just not today." I had become an expert at manipulating Sonja over the years, and I wasn't about to talk about that either. I couldn't pull the trigger. I convinced myself that my behaviors weren't the problem, and I blamed everything on the stress of work. Sonja and I decided we'd take the summer off from Anaheim Vineyard and enjoy a vacation in the desert springs. We even promised our counselor we would make the three-hour drive every Thursday for our sessions with him.

We never made it to vacation. My emotional abuse reached a threshold that caused Sonja to take back all the control I had stripped from her. She snapped in that airport, and I no longer had any control at all.

I had spent years controlling the narrative. I projected who I allowed people to see. I fed off people's enjoyment of my personality. I had fed the people what they wanted too. I had given them all my zeal, energy, passion, and driven-ness and brought my family home crumbs. I had placed everything on the altar of ministry, and now God was claiming it all back.

EXILE

*"God creates out of nothing. Wonderful you say. Yes, to be
sure, but he does what is still more wonderful: he makes
saints out of sinners."*
Søren Kierkegaard, The Journals of Kierkegaard

After my incident with Sonja in the
Minneapolis airport, I knew my life had changed in
an instant. By the time I arrived home, Sonja had
already left to Santa Maria, and the kids were staying
with friends. John sent Todd Hunter to come over
and find out what had happened. I negotiated. I
stalled. I made excuses. Three days later, I resigned.

My wife had left me, but now I also felt
abandoned by my Vineyard family. In my pained
perspective, I felt that everyone pulled back. John
and Carol were determined that I would never set
foot in the pulpit again. They were incredibly hurt by
my actions, but I didn't understand the severity of
their response. Others on staff had struggled in their
marriages. No one in leadership had navigated the
challenges without fault. Nonetheless, the man who
had been my spiritual father for thirty-three years
and had known me since I was a boy suddenly saw
me as harmful to our movement. Days earlier I had
been encouraged, respected, and looked up to by my
peers. Now I was the target of their hostility. I had
nowhere to turn. I realize now that their wagons

were hitched to mine, so when I fell, their sense of security was rocked as well.

When you are in the seat of power, you think you're the guy! None of this would happen if you weren't there. When I was considering the senior pastor role at Anaheim, people had told me I was the only one who could take the position. There was no one else. And I believed them. But it was a trap. As soon as I submitted my resignation, that 747 kept right on flying. All those knobs and buttons I had been pushing for years did nothing. It was all a smokescreen, and I was completely unnecessary to keep that aircraft flying. All of that energy, emotion, and time that I had poured into ministry flew right off without me. And I realized the mistake I had made.

I had lost my ministry, but I was determined to not lose my marriage. I realized Sonja needed a break from me, and I figured a couple weeks away would help clear her head. I continued to meet with our counselor, and he gently warned me that a few weeks were likely not enough to remedy the mess I had made. Sonja had held things in for so long that when the dam finally broke, it tore loose violently. I had tried so hard for years to negotiate control of the marriage, and when she stripped herself loose of that control, she had no filter in how that disdain was expressed. All her imagined fears became her reality. Even though I had never had an affair, she was convinced that I had, and she convinced others as well. I was reaping the rotten fruit of years of trying to control what Sonja did and didn't say.

I was a weepy, pathetic, woe-is-me wreck. I went through all the stages of grief and denial and cycled back through them a thousand times. I was fixated on wanting people to understand my point of view, but no one would listen. And I didn't blame them.

Without my wife, my children, my friends, or my ministry to distract me from my own misery, I was disoriented and helpless. I was a mess. I wandered into a Hollywood Video store one night trying to find a movie that would distract me from my own pain. A man was watching me—short and stalky with a disheveled head of hair. I selected my movie and made my way to the checkout stand.

"You're Carl." The words came from the disheveled head behind me. His kind voice didn't match his appearance.

"Yeah."

"I'm Chubba," he said.

"Okay."

"God told me to take care of you."

What in the world? Surely I have fallen from grace if I have gone from the company of John Wimber to this strange fellow. But over the next few months, Chubba was there for me and my children. He even helped Sonja when she decided to move out of our home. He shut down his business, sent his whole crew to the house, rented the trucks, and moved her to her new place. Chubba became one of the few friends I could rely on in that sore time.

I was sitting in my friend Chris Dewitt's office, slunk into the chair across his desk, crying my eyes out. Chris was at a total loss of what to do for me when Chubba walked in.

"What's the matter, Carl?" came Chubba's sweet inquiry.

"Everything's getting to me, Chubba."

"You need to keep perspective," Chubba implored with kindness. "My brother-in-law's car broke down twice this week."

I looked at Chris and asked, "Who is this guy?!"

"It's Chubba." Enough said. Chris and I glanced at each other and exchanged a knowing smile.

Yes, that was Chubba. He was God's angel to me during those early days and weeks after our separation. He was in my life for a few months, and I will never be able to repay him for the kindness he extended to me and my children.

Other less encouraging voices also had their input. A friend came to me and asked, "What I really want to know is, are you repentant?"

"How would I know?" I responded gruffly. The apparent fact was that I had spent years deceiving myself. Even if I did feel that I was repentant, how did I know that the repentance was authentic? The separation was so fresh. My whole life had just blown up, so I would probably be willing to do anything I needed to do to get it all back together. I would say anything that needed to be said, meet with any counselor, jump through any hoops necessary to rebuild the same house of cards I had before it collapsed. So how could I know if I had truly repented? Repentance takes time.

The first reaction to a life-disrupting situation is to scramble. You do everything you can to control an out-of-control situation. Eventually you scramble so long and so hard that you wear yourself out. The realization slowly sinks in that rebuilding what you had before is futile. Room has to be made for a new normal to develop. You have to take your hands off it, and over time, God shakes out what is real repentance and what's not real. It doesn't really matter what anyone else thinks; God is the only one who can take you deep enough to truly change.

During that scrambling phase, God brought another unexpected friend into my life. Out of the blue, I received a phone call from a man named Ed. He used to be a cocaine addict and had an encounter with the Lord on a night he planned on picking up some coke. He'd dropped by his friend Pam's house to say hi, with the intention of getting drugs later that evening. As he left Pam's home, she handed him a cassette tape of me leading worship. Ed listened to the worship tape, and God crashed in. God encountered Ed and radically saved him from a lifetime of addiction, and my music had played a critical role in that transformation. When he heard about my resignation, he decided to call me. "Carl, I know you don't know me, but I know you. I'm a painter and need some help working on a project. Why don't you join me up in Ketchikan, Alaska? Even if you don't do any work, I'll pay for your hotel to stay up here." No other friends were calling me, so I figured new ones were in order. I didn't have anything better to do, so I flew across the continent to paint houses for a man I had never met.

I landed in Ketchikan and was met by Ed and his brother Larry, who sported an intimidating Fu Manchu mustache and enormous belt buckle. Larry looked me over warily and gave his brother a look that said, "Why the heck did you ask this guy here?" Luckily, I had lots of experience painting houses and I was fast, so it didn't take long for him to warm up to me.

One exhausted evening after a day of painting, we caught the ferry that took us across the river to the town where our hotel was. We stopped at a diner, covered in filth and paint splatters. Our waitress approached, and Ed said, "Hi, Mary. I tell you what. If you can tell me what he does, I'll double your tip," pointing to me. Mary barely knew Ed and knew nothing about me.

She looked at me and confidently declared, "He's a pastor."

We were stunned. *Where did she get that from?* Yet, I held on to that comment as a promise from the Lord that His gifts are without revocation. We stayed in Alaska for a couple of weeks until the painting job was complete; then I headed to Bend, Oregon with Ed and Larry for their next project. The labor was a helpful distraction from the dizzying scrambling I had been doing back in California, so I appreciated the work.

When the work with Ed dried up, I didn't know where else to go. I called my sister, Candy, and she said I could move into her old house, the same one the revival had started in back in 1978. She had kept it over the years as a rental property, and her daughter was currently living there. So I moved back into Candy's house with my niece. The house had been neglected over the years, and it had a leaky roof to prove it. One particularly soggy night, I lamented the fact that I had been at Wimbledon in the VIP seating only a couple months before. Now I was sitting in a dilapidated house trying to stay ahead of the next leak.

I was eventually able to get myself an apartment near the church. Ironically, the apartment complex was called The Vineyard Apartments. I was sitting alone in that apartment when I received a call from Dave Owen on November 17, 1997. John had suffered a brain hemorrhage and died.

I was in shock. I mourned alone. I wept—for everything I had gained from my relationship with the most important man in my life, and everything I had lost. The spiral of grief gripped me again, and I was utterly alone. I became severely depressed.

I received another phone call, this time from Ed. I sobbed into the receiver. My incoherent words indicated my grief and just how badly I was losing it. Apparently I scared Ed, because the next morning I went to the grocery store, and when I got back to the apartment, I saw Ed's truck. He had driven a thousand miles and was waiting for me on my apartment doorstep. As soon as he saw me and assessed that I was okay, he hopped in his truck and headed back north.

My wife was gone. My children were living away from me. All my friends had turned from me. And my mentor and father had died. I navigated those weeks and months by barely hanging on with the help of a cocktail of prescriptions for Paxil, Ambien, and some other meds.

I woke up one morning through a haze of medicated sleep to see a giant hole in the carpet of my front room. Next to it was a five-gallon jug of water. Apparently, I must have set my apartment on fire the night before and had enough awareness to put out the fire with the water. I opened the front door to investigate further and discovered an eviction notice plastered to my door. *What happened?!* I was utterly confused. I had no memory of the fire, and absolutely no idea why I would have been evicted. Surely there had been a mistake.

I charged down to the management office where I was greeted with a look of terror from the manager. "What happened?" I asked.

Impatiently, she replied, "Last night, you were going around the complex beating on doors. You were trying to get into peoples' apartments. The police were here and . . ."

"The police came?!" I was befuddled! I had no recollection of any of this.

"Yes," she retorted. "There's a police report. Call them."

I called the police department, and the officer I spoke to knew exactly who I was. The anger in his voice confirmed everything the apartment manager had said.

"Was I drunk?" I asked.

"No, you were coherent the entire time."

I was frightened that I could have behaved so terribly with absolutely no recollection of it. I had been evicted from the Vineyard. Again. I packed up my bags and headed back to my sister's house.

I continued to see my psychologist. I met with our marriage counselor independently, and Sonja agreed to go to sessions with me as well to work on our marriage. I was torn up about the separation and was fixated on getting back together. Our counselor constantly assured me that I needed to give Sonja the space to feel her need. As much as it was contrary to everything inside me, I was willing to fight the only way I could, by backing off.

When Sonja left me in July of 1997, I was convinced that the separation was a temporary necessity, and she would come to her senses in a few weeks. How wrong I was! I hit the ninety-day mark and vented my frustration to my counselor. He tried to temper my expectations. I was still scrambling to rebuild the marriage we had before. When we hit the one-year mark and Sonja was still content to be separated, I was outraged. "If this goes on much longer, I'm done!" I ranted to our counselor.

"Did someone tell you that everything is fixed after a year? There are no time limits!" I recalled that I had been the one begging Sonja for more time a year earlier. All Sonja was doing was wrestling control back for the time I had stolen from her. I wanted a limit, a system, a program. I wanted to regain control. But God wasn't acquiescing.

During one of our counseling sessions together, our counselor asked Sonja, "How have you experienced Carl?"

She unloaded! Every fault, imagined, real, or exaggerated, spewed from her mouth. And in my estimation, it almost all fit in the imagined category.

"But it's not true!" I protested.

Our counselor replied, "I didn't ask her for the truth. I asked her how she experienced you. Can't you just be big enough to listen?"

That's when I started to learn to listen. For the first time in our marriage, I was learning to listen beyond the facts of what Sonja was saying to the feelings behind those words.

It took two years, but Sonja and I eventually got back together. We decided to move into Sonja's house in the desert with the kids and build a new life together. We continued to see our counselor regularly. I had been painting most of the two years during our separation, and I didn't really want to continue in that line of work. I wasn't sure how I would support my family.

I was talking with an old friend from San Luis Obispo when he asked me what I'd like to do. "Well, I'd like to start a worship label, but that takes money I don't have."

"How much will it take?" he asked

"Probably a couple hundred thousand dollars. Maybe two-fifty."

"No," he interjected. "That won't be enough. If you're going to do it, do it right." He then talked to two of his friends, and the three investors promised me 1.2 million dollars to start Sovereign Productions. Amongst all the rumors that had been flying around about me after my resignation were those that claimed I had been stealing money from the church, so this unsolicited gesture of faith in my integrity was healing to me. Before I left the office, he also asked, "How much money are you in the hole now?" I was ashamed to say $50,000. He wrote me a check for the total amount written to Carl Tuttle, not Sovereign Productions. No strings attached. Just God's mercy.

I operated Sovereign Productions and did consulting work with Grace Worship Label while we lived in the desert. After a couple years, we drove up to Fort Collins, Colorado for my son Noah's wedding. Colorado was absolutely stunning, and we liked the idea of being near Noah and his wife. With my consulting work, I could live anywhere. So we decided to move up to Fort Collins in 2002.

We started attending Vineyard Church of the Rockies, pastored by Rick Olmstead. Rick was incredibly supportive of me, and it wasn't long before I was involved in worship and teaching. I was pastor on call for the congregation, and I really enjoyed being involved in ministry again. Rick tried to intervene with Vineyard USA leadership for me to be officially restored to the movement. When that opportunity fell through at the last minute, I spun into another dark depression. I was still scrambling to rebuild what I used to have in the Vineyard, and God wasn't having it. It felt like every time there was an opportunity to be reconciled or in any way recognized in the movement, something else came up. Another concerned voice would chime in with its objections, and the rug was pulled out from me once again. I experienced heartache after heartache because I longed so much to be recognized as part of the Vineyard again. I had done everything my counselors had asked from me, and I even had a written recommendation from our counselor to support that. Yet, no matter how hard I tried, I still remained exiled from the movement I helped start. I thought I was under church discipline, and I was bewildered why it was taking so long. I didn't realize that it was the Lord's discipline I was under. He operates outside of human timeframes and expectations, and He had other plans for me. Even though I was living in Colorado, He still had me in His desert.

By all outward appearances, Sonja and I were making it. But that's how our marriage had always been. We had never thrived together, and we were never truly happy as a couple. The time in Colorado was no exception. Sovereign Productions had folded, and I still had some royalty income, but I was scrambling to find work to support my family by painting houses.

Despite the marriage, financial, and depression difficulty, God met me in some very amazing ways during my time in Colorado. On one Sunday evening, I decided to visit a charismatic church called Resurrection Church. Worship was outstanding, and I sobbed in the tangible presence of God in that place. I was walking out the door after worship when I heard the pastor introduce the guest speaker for the night, Brennan Manning. That got my attention! I had been reading several of Brennan Manning's books about the unending mercy of God. I had had trouble with the books, not on a theological level, but just because Brennan understood God's love in a way I knew I didn't. It was so real and practical. The sobbing that began in worship continued as I was wrecked by God's love poured out through Brennan Manning. It was a lifeline for me in the midst of a very dark and hopeless place.

Another moment of hope came when I drove up to Colorado Springs to see Ted Haggard (this was when he was still pastoring New Life Church and leading the National Association of Evangelicals). I was desperate and looking for encouragement from any source. Sovereign Productions and Grace Label had ended, and I was barely making it on my painting income. As I left Ted's office, he handed me a folder with the US presidential seal on it. Inside was an envelope with $3,000 in it.

God's reckless mercy intervened again in a movie theater, of all places. I had taken my kids to see *Shrek 2* when I could feel someone staring at me. I turned around to see Steve Collins, a man I had known since 1983. He used to be John's traveling secretary, and Steve and I had laughed our way through the 1984 London trip together. I was bewildered at why I would be seeing him in a movie theater in Ft. Collins, Colorado. It was wonderful to reconnect with him. Steve became a great friend to me during that time, and he gave me painting work to do. He continued to be there for me for the next several years.

In the fall of 2004, I went to a routine checkup with my doctor when she asked why I was still taking Paxil. I explained the major panic attacks I started having in 1995 and how those had ceased with Paxil. She recommended I transition off the Paxil and start taking an antidepressant in its place. She gave me a transition plan to mitigate the withdrawal effects from the Paxil, which I followed precisely. Nonetheless, the transition was brutal on me. I spun even deeper into depression. My emotions were out of control, and I withdrew from everyone. I didn't feel like myself at all.

One evening, I was talking with Sonja, explaining to her how difficult this medication withdrawal was on me. I was a broken, sobbing mess. "Sonja, if you didn't have to be married to me, would you be?"

"No," was her short but honest answer.

"Okay, Sonja. Then you don't have to be. It's okay."

And that was it. Our marriage was over. I packed up my things and moved into a tiny studio apartment in December of 2004.

Christmas came. I was sitting alone in the dark in my studio apartment. No children. No family. No hope. Only darkness and loneliness remained. Everything that ever mattered to me had been stripped away. "God," I cried out, "everything is gone. And I don't know if I can make it."

I could sense a gentle presence. It was as if Jesus was kneeling down at my chair in front of me. He placed his hand on my knee and said, "But I'm here."

For years, I had propped myself up with ministry, position, influence, popularity, and recognition. I had used them to tell me that I was important and worthy of God's love. They were my proof that I was somebody and God cared about me. But now they were all gone. My ministry, my family—it was all gone. They had all vanished. They had all promised so much but delivered nothing but emptiness. In the middle of all that shame, no one remained but Jesus. There He was. And I knew what I had longed for all those years—that He was enough.

From that moment on, things started to change. My situation was the same. My wife was still divorcing me, I was living in a tiny apartment away from my kids, and I was broke. But I knew Jesus was with me, and that was all that mattered.

I received a phone call from a friend in the desert in March 2005. "Why don't you come down here to the desert?" he asked.

"What will I do?" I asked in reply.

"I've got work for you. Just come down here." So I packed my bags and sobbed my way down to the desert. My oldest son was in Southern California, but I was leaving five of my children behind in Colorado. Steve Collins paid for my hotel for me to have a temporary place to stay when I arrived.

Hard labor is a good accompaniment for a broken heart. I arrived to the desert to find the work was in a lumberyard. I was moving hundreds of massive beams and removing all the sharp edges. I put my head down and set to work, not knowing what I was going to be paid. I worked all day and plopped my exhausted body onto the bed some friends were letting me use in their home. I continued working and started renting a room from some acquaintances. I just wanted to go to work, eat, and get from the car to my bed without talking to anybody.

I missed my children tremendously, and that hurt was compounded by the fact that Sonja was excluding me from their lives. She wouldn't let me know if they were sick or having a rough time at school. I had left her a couple checkbooks, so she was always the first to get money when I was paid, but other than that, I had very little contact with my family. I even missed the birth of my first grandchild.

I was also isolated from church and ministry. *If this is it*, I thought to myself, *if I never regain traction in ministry again, it's okay. I've already done more than I ever thought I could do. I've had more privilege, influence, and opportunity than I ever thought. If that's all over and gone and I'm never involved in ministry again, I'll be all right. Jesus is enough.*

One day, I received a call from Mike Mumey, an old friend I had known before I married Sonja. "What are you up to?" he asked.

"I'm out in the desert working."

"Really? Where in the desert?"

"I'm in LaQuinta."

"You're kidding! Karen and I live in Indian Wells, right down the road from LaQuinta."

I hopped into the car to meet them, glad to visit lifelong friends. The vast difference between their lives and mine was apparent from the moment I arrived at their private gated community. We laughed and reminisced our way through dinner and made plans to get together the next night. Before long, we were hanging out together every night. We would cry together, laugh together, and love each other. I told them my story. They told me theirs. They were a safe haven for me.

Our conversations were so fun and life giving, but Karen thought we needed an intervention. One evening, she walked in with a red ball. "You have to hold this ball if you want to talk." We tossed that ball around all night long, talking and laughing our way through the evening. With every pass of the ball, I could feel myself healing.

Then during one of our uproarious evenings together, they ruined it. "I have an idea," Mike said. "Let's go to church."

I was stunned. "Let's not," I protested. But I was outnumbered, so we visited nearby Faith Community Church. Mike and Karen loved it. I wasn't too impressed. Nonetheless, we started attending Faith Community together regularly.

It was a young church, and no one there knew me, which was incredibly refreshing. It was my first glimpse of life outside the Vineyard. Before long the pastor asked me, "Carl, would you like to start leading worship?"

"No, thank you."

"We'll pay you."

"Okay, I'm in." But just to be clear on the terms, I added, "I'm only doing this for the money. I don't want to get involved. I don't want to get to know your people. I just want to show up, lead worship, get my paycheck, and get out. Understand?" Unbelievably, they accepted my terms.

Other than my worship side deal, my primary income was through painting. Usually I worked on new homes before the AC had been installed, not an easy task in the summer in the Southern California desert. On one particularly brutal summer afternoon, I was miserable as I sprayed lacquer in a new home. I picked up my phone and called Ron Worrell, the man who had taught me how to paint three decades earlier. "Ron, I just want you to know this is all your fault!"

"What do you mean?"

"I'm sanding floors and applying lacquer in 115 degrees. And I just wanted to call and say thank you." And I meant it. I was overwhelmed with thankfulness that I had a trade I could use to provide for my family. It was the only link I had to them, and with every sweaty day under paint-dripped clothes and desert sun, I was able to care for my kids the only way I knew how.

I kept getting words that God wasn't through with me yet. At first, that seemed like a scary thought. I had already been through so much. But then I realized it was good news that God wasn't done with me. I continued attending Faith Community Church, and before long I was doing more than just leading worship. I started leading a small group in Mike and Karen's home. Then I was leading outreaches. Before long, I was over all the small groups. I even found myself visiting people in the hospital and taking on more pastoral care. After three years, painting gave way to a full-time ministry position at Faith Community.

"What's happened God?" I prayed. "What have You done?! I'm back in ministry, and I'm really, really in! I'm up to my eyeballs in ministry!" I was stunned at the transformation that had been slowly taking place.

I said to the Lord, "Okay, if I'm back in, then I'm all in. My kids are grown. I'm not married. So take all of this. Take all the years of experience, all the knowledge, all the failures, all the gifts. It's all yours. I want You to use me up."

RETURN TO VINEYARD FAMILY

*"You don't choose your family. They are God's gift to you,
as you are to them."*
Desmond Tutu

*"This is your family. You will spend the rest of your days
with them."*
Holy Spirit to Carl at a Vineyard Conference in 2013

In 2011, I was driving in Brea, about an hour's drive north of my home in the desert, when I happened to notice a man that used to be on staff with me at Anaheim Vineyard crossing the street. He was walking into a church called Southlands. *Interesting*, I thought to myself.

Southlands had Sunday evening services, so I started attending them and met the pastor, Alan Frow, as well as Chris Weinard. They reminded me very much of the Vineyard family in that they were committed to a Word and Spirit emphasis. Something in their church resonated with my roots, and I was drawn to them.

Southlands held a conference called Urban Renewal, and I decided to bring a bunch of people from the desert to attend with me. Mike Pilavachi, the featured speaker, preached about the desert season. Throughout the sermon, I could sense God stirring my heart. At the conclusion of the sermon,

Mike called people forward who were ending a desert period. I knew that my time in the desert was over—both metaphorically and physically.

I left my desert home in April 2012 and moved to Brea where Southlands Church was located. After turning in my resignation at Faith Community Church, I made plans to start painting for a living again. I felt like the Lord said to me, "On your way to Southlands, go to England." England wasn't exactly on the way, and I wondered how I was going to afford an international trip. I hadn't been to the UK since 1997, and I didn't know where I would go or what I would do in England. Soon after this prompting from the Spirit, I received a phone call from a lawyer saying he had a check for me from England for £3500, roughly $5000. So I made plans to spend May of 2012 in England, ministering in churches and homes throughout the UK. It was a time of reconnecting with old friends and a time of refreshing for me as I launched into ministry once again.

After my return from England, I settled into Brea and was ready to jump in as a full-on member of Southlands. I met with Alan Frow, and he cautioned me to tame any expectations. "It would be a long time before you'd be considered for eldership here. I want you to know that before you become too involved."

"I've had position, and I'm not interested in that anymore. It didn't work out so well last time. But

I do know this—if God grants me favor in your community, then you won't call evil what God calls good. I'm fine either way."

As a new member to Southlands, I did what all the new members did. I attended membership class and small groups. I then participated in their small group leadership training. I even signed up for their two-year ministry school course alongside a crowd of twenty-somethings. Alan asked me, "Why are you doing all this? You've pastored a church ten times our size."

"Well, it's what you do here, right? I'm a part of this church, so I want to learn to do things the way you do them here." Alan was stunned that despite all my pastoral and leadership experience, I was willing to submit to their procedures for leadership development.

Other people at the church would ask me, "Did you really go to the membership class?"

"Yeah."

"Why would you do that?"

"That's the way you do it here."

"We never went to membership class."

"Are you here? You need to go to membership class!"

The leaders of the church expressed appreciation for my involvement and the way I modeled being a part of the body. We eventually became very close friends, and they were incredibly supportive of me. They had seen me in some very dark times and knew all the details of my past, and yet they never failed to recognize that God was doing a restorative work within me. They even gave me a role helping young pastors learn how to preach. I was astounded by their acceptance, because I was keenly aware that they would not have responded in the same way to anyone else in a similar situation. I was offered positions and responsibilities that were never given to non-elders.

Alan went so far as to facilitate a meeting between me and Carol Wimber (now Carol Wong). I hadn't seen Carol since my resignation in 1997. My actions had greatly damaged our relationship, so I wasn't sure what to expect at the meeting. A spirit of grace filled the room when we met, and she and I quickly reconciled. We have been very close since that time.

In 2013, I connected with Robert Crabbe, the pastor of a Vineyard Church called The River. He invited me to a dinner where they honored me as a father in the Vineyard. That event was such a blessing as I was able to reconnect with Carol, Blaine Cook, Ken Fish, and others. It was my first time in seven years to be around the Vineyard since my move from Ft. Collins.

The following year I attended my first Vineyard conference in over a decade. I sat in worship, simply observing it all. I didn't even participate; I was just soaking it all in. A thought overcame me. *The movement is moving again!* It was a delight to witness. Then I heard something unexpected. God spoke to me and said, "This is your family. You will spend the rest of your days with them."

I smiled and said back to the Lord, *You might want to let* them *know.*

Upon my return to Southlands, I told Alan what the Holy Spirit had spoken. I wasn't giving him any options, just relaying what God had said. Alan was bummed. He knew it was true and unselfishly served me as I transitioned back into the Vineyard. Alan is truly the greatest pastor I have ever met.

Robert Crabbe invited me to join him at a Vineyard regional pastors retreat where Jamie Wilson was ministering. Phil Strout, the National Director of Vineyard USA, was also there. Prophetic words were being shared, and Jamie stood to give a word. "I see a tree that has been cut down. But there is a root that is coming up from the tree." I knew the word was for me, and so did everyone around me. I ignored the stares in my direction, including the one coming from Phil. I was not going to budge! I wasn't going to go forward, no matter what. I didn't want to draw attention to myself, because everyone knew who I was, and I didn't want to make anything be about me.

After the service was over, I went back to my cabin, settled in for the night, and checked to see if I was lucky enough to catch any of the internet reception that seemed to be eluding everyone else. Surprisingly, I got a connection and quickly logged onto Facebook. A message popped up. It was from Carol. The short message said, "Job 14:7." Nothing more. I pulled out my Bible and looked it up. "At least there is hope for a tree: If it be cut down, it will sprout again, and its new shoots will not fail."

I was stunned. There was no way even I could misinterpret what God was saying. He had said it twice in the same evening in almost the exact same imagery. I decided that no matter what, I would go forward for prayer the next night. I talked with Phil the next day and told him about the message I had received from Carol. "Even if the altar call tonight is for female problems, I'm going up there," I promised. And that's exactly what I did.

All heaven broke loose. God's sweet presence moved and re-grafted me back into the vine. I knew that I was a part of the Vineyard again, and I never wanted to leave. This was my inheritance, and I wasn't going to let it go. More than my inheritance, this was my family. I belonged to them, and they belonged to me.

2 Samuel 14:14 tells us, "As water is poured out on the ground and cannot return, so we all must die. But God does not take away life, but He devises

ways for the banished one to return." I'd felt banished, like the city of refuge, and I never thought I could come out of exile. But God devised a way in His faithfulness.

In January 2014, I joined the staff of Robert Crabbe's Vineyard church, The River, as an interim pastor. Robert and his wife Teresa entrusted me to lead as they were working through a crisis in the church. I will always be grateful that the Crabbes brought me back into the Vineyard family, and I deeply honor them for it. Eventually, I took on a co-pastor role alongside Don Wheeler. It was very important to me that Vineyard was in the church's name, so we changed the name to Vineyard at the River. I've been serving as co-pastor with Don there ever since.

Every child growing up in a family has to learn his or her own identity, and I went through a similar journey in my Vineyard family experience. Looking back with the perspective of over five decades with Wimber and the Vineyard helped me realize that my identity had manifested as two very different personas. I existed as two different people inside one man, and one of those people was very uncomfortable for a very long time.

From a young age, I received much affirmation, beginning as a teen with John and Carol Wimber, Bob and Penny Fulton, and others, and the affirmation increased as I took on greater roles and responsibilities. That affirmation continued as I was groomed for leadership and eventually ordained with Calvary Chapel. It only increased through the outpouring of God's blessing on the birth and flourishing of the Vineyard moment and Vineyard music. I was granted so much favor, it's ridiculous!

There's nothing wrong with affirmation. It's a gift that, when rightly used, can ground us in identity based on the love and grace of God. However, I became adept at also using that affirmation illegally to prop myself up. God was blessing my life and using me, but I misapplied those gifts as the basis of God's love for me. I became keen to engage in activities that were reciprocated with the most accolades, and I adjusted my behavior to elicit the most approval from others. I became what pleased people. I became what I thought they wanted. They liked my charisma and over-the-top personality, so I gave it right back to them in spades.

When I stepped up on a stage, I was bold and passionate, funny, and articulate. News flash: I'm not really those things. Or at the least, I'm not fully those things. I'm not a people person at all. Sometimes I rather dislike people. The man who was brought to his knees by panic attacks still lives inside me, and when I see a crowd of people, my first response is to be overcome with social anxiety. I feel obligated to know everybody and be something for them.

A different metamorphosis would happen as I stepped off the stage, drove home from church, and walked into my home. Rather than being engaged and active, I immediately became quiet, sullen, and dark. I was split. I was a different person alone, and that person was so unhappy with himself that he sometimes numbed that pain in unhealthy ways. The two parts of myself could never be in the same room. Exuberant Carl 1 pretended shame-filled Carl 2 didn't exist, and Carl 2 had to ignore God's goodness and mercies that were so evident in Carl 1's life. Arrogance and defensiveness were my shield; deflection and minimizing were my weapons.

Many of my efforts over the years had been undertaken to prevent people from looking behind the Wizard of Oz's curtain to see who really lurked behind. I was so good at it that I didn't even allow myself a peek.

The growth that only comes through heartbreak and loss has taught me a different way to live. Now, rather than finding comfort in a stage persona, I have become incredibly uncomfortable with any sense of putting on one thing to become another in any setting. I am charismatic—that part of my personality was evident before I ever had prominence and it will stay long after a spotlight fades. But I'm also a lot more laid back about it now than I was twenty years ago. I don't need the stage. I don't need the title. I just need Jesus, and that's all that matters.

Shame haunted me my whole life from my childhood, through my ordination in 1978, and into my demise in 1997. A few years ago, I came across author and speaker Brené Brown. She is a sociologist and researcher of shame and its effects. She explains that vulnerability is a primary tool we can use to combat shame. She states, "I spent a lot of years trying to outrun or outsmart vulnerability by making things certain and definite, black and white, good and bad. My inability to lean into the discomfort of vulnerability limited the fullness of those important experiences that are wrought with uncertainty: Love, belonging, trust, joy, and creativity to name a few."

I spent the first four and a half decades of my life outrunning my own shame, and the last few years have been spent leaning into the vulnerability that comes with trying to face it head on. What I so longed for before—love, belonging, trust, and joy—were completely elusive when I was scrambling to control the narrative of my life and the way people perceived me.

I wish so badly that I had turned to Jesus rather than away from Him, for all those years. But I didn't. I placed all my confidence in the approval of others, so when all of that disappeared, I was left with nothing. Many people rightfully reacted very negatively to my failures. I hadn't been honest with them, and so it's only natural that I began to reap what I had sown. My resignation left questions, and it's natural that those questions were met with all sorts of speculations. Rumors abounded, including that I was a pedophile, I beat my wife and children, and I stole from the church. People's need to place blame overshadowed the fact that the rumors were all fictitious and without merit. The blame was placed on the right person but with the wrong particulars. But that's the kind of thing that goes on when you fail as a leader, and I became victim to my own game. Christians shot their wounded, but I supplied the ammo!

About a decade after my exile began, I received an email one night from a person I had known very well in the Vineyard who hadn't reacted all that well to my failures. She had been responsible for believing and spreading many false accusations about me. She wrote to me that while she was meeting with some friends, I had been mentioned as a topic of prayer. One of the people present had a vision, and they interpreted it to mean that God wasn't through with me yet.

As I read the letter, none of this was news to me. I knew God still had mercy for me. However, God's mercy toward me was a revelation to these folks. Such revelation came with no mention of regret for their actions toward me or any pain that they had caused through false rumors or rejection. Their surprise at God's goodness toward me pierced me once again and brought back fresh memories of feeling betrayed and abandoned. I turned my gaze from the computer screen to my ceiling. "Lord, what do I do with this?!" The pain felt as fresh as it had been a decade earlier.

As I looked back to the screen, suddenly I could see Luke 6:28-36 superimposed on my monitor:

"Bless those who curse you, pray for those who mistreat you. If someone slaps you on one cheek, turn to them the other also. If someone takes your coat, do not withhold your shirt from them. Give to everyone who asks you, and if anyone takes what belongs to you, do not demand it back. Do to others as you would have them do to you. If you love those who love you, what credit is that to you? Even sinners love those who love them. And if you do good to those who are good to you, what credit is that to you? Even sinners do that. And if you lend to those from whom you expect repayment, what credit is that to you? Even sinners lend to sinners, expecting to be repaid in full. But love your enemies, do good to them, and lend to them without expecting to get anything back. Then your reward will be great, and you will be children of the Most High, *because he is kind to the ungrateful and wicked*" (emphasis mine).

My heart sunk at that last phrase. I was struck with the realization that "the ungrateful and wicked" described me to a tee. Somberness flooded me as the Lord whispered to me, "Carl, they don't owe you anything." It didn't matter what they had said or done; Jesus had already picked up the tab. I no longer had to blame anyone else for my exile. I didn't hold anyone else responsible for my abandonment.

Within the darkness of my exile from the Vineyard, I had no hope of ever returning. Only Jesus could have performed such a miracle. All my attempts, and even the attempts of others on my behalf, to reconcile and reunite me to the Vineyard over the years had come to naught. I don't take for granted the blessing I now walk in with my Vineyard family. I had made a mess of things. God was the only one who could unscramble scrambled eggs. All my scrambling just made bigger messes. His brought unity and peace.

For years, I thought I was under church discipline. I had disappointed the church, so I was being held at arm's length from it. I've come to realize that church discipline as we experience it is pretty inadequate. It offers an outline of what you need to do according to a secular approach to healing and restoration. If you correct outward behavior, man will sign off.

However, if you are under the Lord's discipline, no amount of hoop-jumping or behavior modification will remove you from that discipline. He is a good Father, and therefore He disciplines us. He knows us in our deepest, darkest parts. When I realized that my return to the Vineyard wasn't being delayed by men but by God, I realized I was in serious trouble. Man relents, but God doesn't.

People are going to believe what they want to believe; it's a waste of time trying to correct it all. God's pleasure is the only one we ought to pursue, and He can take care of the rest of it. My affirmation and identity must stem from abiding in His love and presence, not what anyone else has to say about me. Because of my songwriting, I'm known around the world. I still receive mail from people telling me how wonderful I am. That's nice, but it's not exactly true. I appreciate it, but don't believe it, because they don't know me. In the same way that I don't take flattery too seriously, I also don't blindly swallow the opinions of those who have chosen to believe the worst about me. That's not true either. I can't be characterized by either of those polar opposites.

Figure out who you are, and just be that. There are always going to be people who are better at doing what you do, and with today's access to teaching and worship online, it can become easy to aspire to be something we aren't. Rather than emulating what God is doing in someone else, just be who God made you to be. Only Bethel can be Bethel, only Vineyard can be Vineyard, and so on. Settle into the vulnerability of enjoying being you rather than being a cheap imitation of someone else.

Personalities are complex, and none of us are one thing all of the time. The trouble comes when we become one thing in public and another thing privately. Seek to surround yourself with those who accept your flaws and your gifts and don't think too highly of either. If you're only accepted when you are acceptable, the temptation will be to modify your behaviors to try and be acceptable. Living for the approval of others is a cruel taskmaster.

I'm convinced that God's grace is up for the task. Paul says, "The grace of God has appeared to all men and it teaches us to say no to ungodliness and worldly pleasure" (Titus 2;11-12). How can we know that we have been affected by the grace of God? Do we love what He loves and hate what He hates? Can we say no to the poison of the world? Can we say no to feeding the beast of shame and instead turn our affections to Him?

I have found that a good measure of how well I'm partaking of the grace God has for me is to ask myself, *Do I love what He loves?* God loves people! Muslim people, atheist people, drunkards, and immoral people. Do I love them all? As long as I allow myself to have distain or disgust toward others' sins, I really don't know my own sin. It was my sin that drove those nails in His hands and thrust that spear in His side. It was my voice that rang out, "Crucify Him!" My sin has never surprised God. Other people, yes. Myself, yes. But never God. Understanding that might make us a nicer people—a kinder, gentler tribe.

Our God is a redeemer and a restorer, and He loves to make things right. It seems almost wrong to say this, but I love my life. I don't deserve it, but I'm at peace and happy. I love my children and grandchildren, and they love me. And I love my Vineyard family. Ministry is not who I am; it's what I do. Who I am is His child who is beloved.

I came into the Vineyard as a kid. Now I've returned to it as a father. I look to the future with anticipation and hope and in the company of family. As God's grace continues to transform me, I want to be everything He's called me to be. I want to devote the rest of my days to my kids and grand-kids and, as John taught me, to loving Christ, His church, and His cause. I recognize the church has its faults, but I love it nonetheless. I love the mission of Jesus. He came down to us where we are. He walked among us in our filth. He is the God who comes down. He's not unattainable. He came down to Zaccheus and the woman at the well. He touched lepers and the unclean. He came down and touched me.

I am a recipient of God's reckless mercy. Rather than being disqualified, I am actually more positioned now to see lives changed. Telling the truth about myself allows people to tell the truth about themselves. I've been able to walk others through journeys similar to mine and to stand as a father to those coming up behind me in the hope that they don't have to make some of the same mistakes I've made. 1997 was the culmination of reaping what I had been sowing for the previous four decades. Now I am beginning to reap the fruit of what I have sown throughout the last few years. Now others are able to eat from the harvest of what God has done in my life, and it's a joy to observe.

I'm change in His pocket and He can spend me however He wants. And He does. So one day I may be in England ministering to crowds of thousands. Another day, I might be praying alongside a baby's hospital bed. Another day may find me in a coffee shop with a pastor, letting him pour his heart out to me. Or I might be painting a house. But it doesn't matter. All that matters is that I am His, and I don't need anything else. He is enough.

AFTERWORD

This might sound strange, but knowing that you have reached this page makes me very uncomfortable—because it means you've read my story—and now you know.

Writing this book has been a process of getting real with myself, and letting others read it has been a process of becoming completely vulnerable.

It's no secret to me that I maintained different personas throughout much of my life; but for so long, I did a really good job keeping them separate. Some of you were personally a part of various stories written in this book, and your memories might bear a different reality than mine. You may have experienced only one version of me, whereas I am aware of multiple personas—pastor, abuser, songwriter, controller, worship leader, etc. The stark contrast is still hard for me to stomach. There's truly nothing more uncomfortable than being "in the same room" as all the different people I've been throughout the years. It's brutal to allow the pastor and the abuser, the worship leader and the controller, to step into the same space. Yet, on these pages, every version of me has finally collided into one very real, very raw, very messy story.

I honestly cringed as I reread certain pages of this manuscript. Chapter one was especially excruciating for me. The way I used to behave makes me want to crawl out of my own skin and perhaps it makes you feel the same.

However, I have chosen not to hide who I was then or who I am now. My desire in writing this book was to be wholly transparent. No matter how uncomfortable it makes you or makes me, I have to be honest about my story. *Because unless I own it, it will own me.*

Taking responsibility for my mistakes and being honest with myself is where I've found freedom. If I don't choose to be vulnerable, maybe you won't either. If I don't own my mess, maybe you won't own yours. I've laid my faults bare before you in the hopes that you will do the same. Will it make you uncomfortable? Yes. But ultimately, it will set you free.

Today, I am a free man. And I'm a man who knows God's mercy. In fact, it is the grace of God that has taught me to say no to ungodliness and worldly pleasure. It's just taken a lot longer than I thought it would. But that's my journey, and you have your own unique journey to walk out.

Finally, I want to close with this. As you've now read, there were times in my past when I felt isolated, lonely, and abandoned. However, I now know that the reality is that I never was actually alone. I've had dozens upon dozens of people who have been *with me* and *for me* throughout my process. In fact, there are so many people that I won't attempt to name them all. But those who have walked with me know who they are. On this final page, allow me to say "thank you." I am grateful to each person who has been a part of my journey.

Thanks for reading my story. May God bless you as your own unfolds.

OTHER BOOKS BY COACHING SAINTS

FROM THE SANCTUARY TO THE STREETS: INSIGHTS AND ADVENTURES IN POWER EVANGELISM
BY CHARLES BELLO AND BRIAN BLOUNT

From the Sanctuary to the Streets is a practical guide written to propel the reader into a lifestyle marked by intimacy with God and power evangelism. Through teaching and personal stories, the authors share with humor and honesty their own efforts to embrace the empowering activity of the Holy Spirit. As the authors state, "We are not called to be spiritual recluses or trail blazing burnouts. Rather, we are called to be friends of God who live a life of intimacy and impact as we simply do life with God in a naturally supernatural way."

PRAYER AS A PLACE: SPIRITUALITY THAT TRANSFORMS
BY CHARLES BELLO

Prayer as a Place is an invitation to partner with Christ as he leads the believer into the dark places of his or her own heart. The purpose of this journey is to bring holiness and wholeness to the child of God. With candor and brutal honesty, Pastor Charles Bello shares his own reluctance and then resolve to follow Christ on this inward journey. In sharing his story, readers gain insight into what their own personal journeys may look like. *Prayer as a Place* reads like a road map as it explores the contemporary use of contemplative prayer as a means of following Christ inward.

FOR MORE TITLES, VISIT:
WWW.COACHINGSAINTS.COM

CPSIA information can be obtained
at www.ICGtesting.com
Printed in the USA
FSOW04n1007250917
39097FS